Praise for *By Bread Alone*

By Bread Alone is a soulful, searching glimpse into trusting the goodness of God when it seems most opaque. Kendall Vanderslice trades toxic positivity for the promise of sustenance, and the result is deeply honest and curiously comforting. These pages are dusted with the flour of daily bread. If you are lost, longing, hope-weary, or barely hanging on (aren't we all?), read this and be nourished.

SHANNAN MARTIN
Author of *Start with Hello* and *The Ministry of Ordinary Places*

I am grateful for Kendall Vanderslice's *By Bread Alone*—a sustenance of hope, a needed nourishment for us hungering to create beauty faced with the bitter gaps of our divided cultures. Her words give rise to our tenderness, and her memorable chapters fill our hearts with compassion. Every page of this book (full of recipes) is brimming with refractive colors shining through the broken prisms of her life, a communion journey of service in tears, as a sojourner baker, a fellow maker into the aroma of the new.

MAKOTO FUJIMURA
Artist and author of *Art + Faith: A Theology of Making*

In this deeply personal account, baker-theologian Kendall Vanderslice explores how baking bread can become a lens through which we understand the Eucharist anew and what it means to allow God to form our lives into a living sacrifice for the life of the world. Be moved, touched, and inspired as you journey with Kendall into the world of artisan bread, embodiment, and what it means to fully embrace your vocation.

GISELA KREGLINGER, PhD
Author of *The Spirituality of Wine* and *The Soul of Wine*

By Bread Alone provides a refreshing perspective on the intersection between faith and food. Kendall eloquently uses her baking expertise and experience to poignantly remind us that the simple acts of making, breaking, and eating bread have profound theological implications.

ADRIAN MILLER
James Beard Award winner and executive director of the Colorado Council of Churches

By Bread Alone is a powerful invitation into the rhythms of baking and the rhythms of faith. As Kendall explains, these are complex journeys of nuance and transformation that mirror each other. Through a robust exploration of breadmaking and her own story, Kendall vulnerably and insightfully offers an alternative to the "Wonder Bread theology" that often plagues the church. This book nourishes and satisfies our deepest longings for the Bread of Life.

KAT ARMAS
Author of *Abuelita Faith* and host of *The Protagonistas* podcast

By Bread Alone is a tender and vulnerable story of Kendall's search to be satisfied by God's provision for her given life. A memoir about what it means to be hungry, what it means to be filled, and what it means to not always get what you desire. I loved this book and needed it myself. Every woman who has struggled to love and learn and lean into their body while still looking with hope toward their resurrected body needs this book.

LORE FERGUSON WILBERT
Author of *A Curious Faith* and *Handle with Care*

Bake & Pray

BAKE & PRAY

Liturgies & Recipes for Baking Bread as a Spiritual Practice

KENDALL VANDERSLICE

TYNDALE
MOMENTUM

A Tyndale nonfiction imprint

Visit Tyndale online at tyndale.com.

Visit Tyndale Momentum online at tyndalemomentum.com.

Visit the author at kendallvanderslice.com.

Designed by Julie Chen

Edited by Stephanie Rische

The author is represented by Alive Literary Agency, www.aliveliterary.com.

The URLs in this book were verified prior to publication. The publisher is not responsible for content in the links, links that have expired, or websites that have changed ownership after that time.

For information about special discounts for bulk purchases, please contact Tyndale House Publishers at csresponse@tyndale.com, or call 1-855-277-9400.

Library of Congress Cataloging-in-Publication Data

A catalog record for this book is available from the Library of Congress.

ISBN 978-1-4964-6138-4

Printed in China

30	29	28	27	26	25	24
7	6	5	4	3	2	1

*In honor of the women throughout history and
around the world who have known God in the
simple rhythms of baking their daily bread*

Contents

Introduction

THE CLOCK ON MY CAR'S DASHBOARD READ 3:42 A.M. as I pulled out of my parking spot on Marion Street. I drove past the school before turning left onto Kirkland and heading toward Harvard Square.

Boston—or, technically, Cambridge-Somerville—is a tough city for a single woman in her early twenties trying to get her feet under her. The weather is intense. The cost of living is high. The people are driven. I loved it, and I was perpetually exhausted and intimidated.

At this hour, though, the edge dulled. The city was silent. The streets were empty. The students who were on their way to become the next generation of judges, senators, and CEOs were sleeping, as every human has to do. I breathed slowly and deeply through the drive.

A few minutes later, I pulled up next to Sofra Bakery. I unlocked the door, turned on the lights, and flipped the switch to preheat the ovens. The muted roar of fans filled the space.

Soon the rest of the bakers would arrive, and we would chat around the big wooden table while weighing flour and brushing butter onto phyllo dough. Not long after, the front-of-house staff would walk in, and the rush to open would begin.

For the rest of the day, the bakery would be loud and busy. Space would be tight. I would rush up and down the back stairs carrying fifty-pound bags of flour and sugar or giant bins filled with dough.

But first I had an hour on my own—an hour of total silence to pull scones, morning buns, and brioche from the walk-in cooler and prepare them for baking.

In that silence, my movements slowed and I sensed the nearness of God. I prayed through hard decisions and complicated friendships, through job opportunities and painful moments at church. On Sundays, I rushed from the bakery to church, receiving Communion week after week with bread dough still stuck to my arms.

The dough in my hands at work, as well as the bread pressed into my palm at church, were tangible reminders that God was with me and that God cared.

Five years later, when I opened my own little bakery in the basement of a popsicle shop in Durham, North Carolina, the memory of those early-morning prayers came rushing back. By that point I had worked for a church, helping them build a bakery to support their ministry, and I'd written a book on the ways God meets us at the table. I'd gotten degrees in food studies at Boston University and in theology at Duke—all driven by the desire to understand how and why I sensed God so palpably in the kitchen. I learned a lot along the way. But no amount of reading or studying or writing could compare to the process of baking itself as a form of prayer.

No matter where you are on your baking journey or your prayer journey, God wants to meet *you* in the kitchen as well. Whether you've been baking for years or you're just learning, whether you've been praying for your whole life or you're just exploring to see what it's all about, this book was written with you in mind.

I have been teaching the Bake & Pray method in churches and schools across the United States and Canada since 2016, helping others discover God's nearness as they mix and shape dough. It is my greatest joy to watch people emerge from that workshop with confidence in their baking skills and with new appreciation for the importance of bread in the story of Scripture and the history of the church.

As you follow the steps to bake bread, and as you learn about the various processes at work along the way, you will learn something about the character of God and the life of faith. I hope that in the baking, you sense God's presence, provision, and promise—and God's incredible creativity as well. I hope you discover that baking bread and praying, together, each enrich the other. And I hope that, over time, baking as a spiritual practice will draw you into closer relationship with God while expanding your appreciation for the global and historical nature of Christ's church—the body made one in the breaking of bread.

THE SACRED LANGUAGE OF BREAD

All throughout Scripture, bread serves as a sign of God's blessing. It marks God's presence and provision, as well as God's promises to us. Bread is a narrative tool God uses to tell us the story of God's work in the world.

To fully understand the scope of this story, we need to start with the very first mention of bread in Scripture, in Genesis 3:19: "By the sweat of your brow you shall eat *bread,* until you return to the ground, from which you were taken; for you are dust, and to dust you shall return" (emphasis added).

Prior to this point in Genesis, Adam and Eve had been fed by the fruits of the trees. Their job was to tend to and enjoy God's creation, and their only restriction was to stay away from the fruit of one tree, the tree of the knowledge of good and evil. In the end, they gave in to temptation, and they plucked from the forbidden tree and ate. By Genesis 3:19, they were learning the repercussions of their disobedience. One such repercussion? That the soil would sprout forth thistles and thorns, and the production of food would require an incredible amount of work.

Bread does not grow on a tree. You can't just pick it and eat. In order to have bread, you need to grow wheat, harvest it, thresh it, and then grind it into flour. It requires you to mix up dough and let it ferment and grow. You need to chop wood to maintain a fire and then bake the dough before finally being able to eat. The production of bread requires an incredible amount of labor and a long series of transformations. This labor is the heartbreaking reality expressed in Genesis 3:19.

At the same time, all this labor and transformation results in a food that contains most of the nutrients needed to survive. And it's something quite delicious, as well. I think it's fascinating that the first mention of bread in Scripture comes alongside these statements about the Curse. Since the beginning, bread has been a blessing from God offered to humanity even in the face of a broken creation.

All throughout Scripture, God provides bread in a manner that relieves God's people for just a moment from the pain of the Curse, from the sweat of their brow by which they eat their food.

In the story of the Israelites' journey through the wilderness, God provided bread that didn't require this extensive labor. Today, we can just run to our local bakery or grocery store to pick up a loaf of bread whenever we get the hankering for it. Or if we have the patience and want to bake it ourselves, we can pick up the flour on demand and turn our ovens to the needed temperature. But for the Israelites, the provision of manna every morning was a reprieve from a great amount of labor—work that was impossible when they were wandering through the desert and unable to grow and harvest grain. All the Israelites had to do was go out and gather the manna each morning. They received bread as a blessing without the toil required in Genesis 3.

And, of course, they had to trust every day that God would continue to provide.

The feeding of the five thousand mirrors this miraculous provision. Jesus multiplied five loaves to feed thousands of people—with baskets and baskets of leftovers. The people who were fed through this miracle likely understood how much labor was required to grow and harvest and grind enough grain to make this quantity of bread. They knew how much strength was needed to mix and knead and shape the loaves.

At the very least, the disciples had a sense for how much labor was circumvented through the miraculous provision of bread. "It would take more than half a year's wages to feed this crowd!" the disciples told Jesus in Mark's account of the story.

Like the Israelites in the desert, the people in the crowd were witnesses to God's miraculous provision through bread freed from the Curse.

On the night before his death, when Jesus offered his own body to his disciples as bread, he took this story one step further.

Jesus did not give them bread that offered momentary relief from the Curse. It wasn't just the labor of growing and harvesting grain that Jesus circumvented in this provision.

It was death itself.

Jesus took the entire curse of sin and death, as well as the labor of defeating death, onto his own body, and then offered that body back to his followers as bread.

The bread Jesus offered his disciples in the upper room, and the bread we are offered every time we celebrate Communion, echoes God's miraculous provision of manna and bread for the five thousand. It serves as a sign of God's presence, like the twelve loaves of showbread the Israelites placed in the Tabernacle. But it is also a promise that God will complete the work begun in the death and resurrection of Jesus.

To this day, bread continues to serve as a picture of both the brokenness and the goodness of creation, though the ways we experience this ache are a bit different from the ways our ancestors did. Very few of us have to physically sweat to make a loaf of bread, but we still feel the effects of the Curse in allergies to gluten, industrialized loaves that make people sick, and wars fought over the distribution of wheat. Bread, for many people, still serves as a reminder that creation is not as God intended it to be.

And yet bread also serves as a promise that God is at work making all things new. For now, we remember this promise in the bread broken at the Communion table, the bread that makes us one as the body of Christ. This Communion bread offers us a taste of the Kingdom of heaven that spreads like leaven throughout the earth. When we go forth from the Communion table and bake the daily breads of our fellow Christians around the world, we taste for a moment the goodness of God's Kingdom, here and now.

From the bread served at the Communion table to our daily bread, and in the relationship between the two, we draw near to God and bear witness to the magnificence of God's beloved creation.

EMBODIED PRAYER

While eating bread can provide a beautiful picture of God's work in the world, this book is not just about eating it. It's about *baking* bread—and baking that bread as a form of prayer. If you've never considered baking as a method of communing with God, the concept might seem strange. But that just means we may need to expand our idea of what it means to pray.

What comes to mind when you think of prayer?

Maybe you are someone who journals your prayers, keeping a log of petitions and answers. Maybe you pray from a prayer book, following the words and rhythms of Christians throughout the ages. Maybe you enjoy praying in community, boldly asking the Holy Spirit to show up.

Or maybe you find prayer intimidating. You don't know what to say to God, or you're not quite sure you believe there is even a God on the other side, taking in your words. Maybe you feel out of practice or you're just tired of praying because it seems like God is silent in return.

Christian tradition has a rich trove of prayer practices to draw from. All too often, though, we assume that prayer is primarily something that happens in our minds. We treat prayer as though it's a mental exercise we go through to stay in touch with God. But what does that mean for the seasons when God doesn't say anything back? What does it mean for the times when God's answers aren't what we want to hear?

God did not make us to be creatures that only think and speak. God created us with bodies that taste and feel and move. These bodies are the primary means by which we get to know creation—just watch any infant who explores the world around them by putting things in their mouth—and they are the primary means by which we get to know our Creator as well. Through our movement, through our senses, we are able to know God and be present with God in a rich way.

"We learn the language of prayer by immersing ourselves in the language that God uses to reveal Himself to us," writes Eugene Peterson, encouraging Christians to not just read Scripture but to immerse ourselves in it as a method of learning to pray.[1] Throughout Scripture, God uses bread as a means of revealing God's character and nature to us, as well as a means of describing God's Kingdom to come. "I am the bread of life," Jesus says in John's gospel.

"The kingdom of God is like yeast that a woman took and mixed into three measures of flour," he says in the Gospels of Matthew and Luke.

On the path to Emmaus, two of Jesus' disciples spent a day in conversation with him and didn't know it was him until he broke the bread.

Christians throughout history have consumed the bread broken at the Communion table and heard the words "Take, eat, this is my body, broken for you." They've made bread to celebrate all kinds of holidays and to mark the changing seasons in the church year.

Bread in these instances is not merely a metaphor. The very chemistry of the baking of bread mirrors God's work in the world. We might say that bread is a form of language through which God speaks to us. And learning the language of bread by actually baking it—paying attention to our senses and moving our hands to mix, shape, bake, and listen to what the bread has to say—is a form of prayer. The process draws us into the presence of God and invites us to know God in a new way. This doesn't require any special tools or tricks beyond what's needed to make an ordinary loaf of bread.

It simply requires us to dwell in the presence of God.

For me, baking is a grounding practice in times when God's whispers are too quiet for me to hear. It is a calming practice when my anxiety threatens to overwhelm me and keeps me from waiting on God. It is a practice that allows me to grieve, celebrate, lament, laugh, and work through the whole host of competing emotions I can feel at any given time. And it continually reminds me of my place in a faith tradition that stretches through history and around the world.

I want bread making to do the same for you.

HOW TO USE THIS BOOK

This book is divided into five parts:

- PART 1: Mise en Place
- PART 2: Basics of Bread
- PART 3: A Liturgy for Bread Making
- PART 4: Recipes for the Church Year
- PART 5: Prayers for Every Occasion

Mise en Place is the practice of preparing yourself and your workspace for the recipe you are about to make. It involves reading the instructions all the way through and then gathering all your ingredients and tools so you don't run out of flour or get surprised by the twelve-hour rest halfway through the process. I like to think of mise en place as a time to prepare my mind and body as well, asking God to be present with me as I bake.

In this first part, I explain *why* I teach the craft of bread baking as a method of prayer. I also provide some background information you will need before you get started. It might be tempting to skip ahead and get right to the baking. But just like in a professional kitchen, this mise en place step helps ensure your success in the process to come.

In part 2, "Basics of Bread," I walk you through six lessons in bread baking. Each lesson includes a theological reflection on the bread-making step at hand and a liturgy-recipe to help you pay attention to the role that step plays in the final loaf.

I recommend that you spend about a week with each lesson. On the first day, read and reflect on the lesson. On the second and third days, bake a loaf of bread using the liturgy-recipe (the process takes up to two days). Record your notes about the loaf in the journaling pages at the back of the book. On the fourth and fifth days, bake a second loaf of bread. Again, record any notes in the journaling pages, paying attention to what you learned from one loaf to the next. Can't eat two loaves of bread in one week? That's okay! This is a great opportunity to share the fruits of your baking with a friend or neighbor.

It might seem like a lot, but this practice should only require about twenty minutes of active time each day. It makes for a perfect morning or evening rhythm of prayer.

If the idea of baking twice a week is just a bit too much for you right now, don't fret. You could stretch out the lessons over the course of two weeks instead, baking one loaf per week. The rationale behind baking twice per lesson is that the repetition helps you more fully understand the bread as well as the practice of baking as a form of prayer.

Perhaps the idea of baking the same style of bread week after week sounds boring. If so, consider the practice as akin to playing scales to learn music or repeating phonetic sounds to learn to read. These basic rhythms will create a solid foundation so you can go on to bake a variety of recipes in the future. Plus, this basic bread is perfect for a variety of uses—it makes delicious toast and sandwiches, as well as a great side for a hearty bowl of soup. Small variations are provided throughout the lessons, so you shouldn't get bored anytime soon!

The next part, "A Liturgy for Bread Making," is designed to help you bake as a form of prayer all through the year, for all kinds of occasions. It includes a basic bread-making liturgy designed to be used at any time, along with a collection of prayers that can be inserted into the liturgy depending on the purpose of your bake.

In part 4, "Recipes for the Church Year," you'll find recipes from around the world associated with each season of the liturgical calendar. This part is designed to help you bake as a form of prayer through each season of the church year while also introducing you to the unique breads and traditions from Christians all around the world. It's a reminder that Christians from this global and historical community are drawn together both in the bread we consume on Sunday morning and the bread we eat throughout the year.

Part 5, "Prayers for Every Occasion," provides a collection of prayers to be used when baking for a wide variety of reasons. This part is meant to help you approach bread making as a time to meet God, no matter the reason for your bake.

At the end you will find a collection of journaling pages. This is a place to note your observations about each loaf of bread and to note observations about yourself as well. The practice will help you grow in awareness of the many variables that affect your final loaf and serve as a record of your own spiritual journey.

PART 1

MISE EN PLACE

Everything in its place

HAVE YOU EVER STARED AT THE ROWS OF COOKBOOKS in the bookstore or the thousands of recipes online and wondered how to choose the right one? Have you ever compared techniques from one source to the next, with each author adamant about their particular method yet all contradicting one another?

Bread making can be overwhelming! It's hard to know where to begin. Over the past few decades, crusty European-style loaf breads have gained popularity in the United States, as has the quest to perfect this complex technique. The result is a wide variety of teaching styles and a bread-making culture that can be intimidating to step into.

The truth is, there is so much flexibility in bread making that many different methods of teaching work. Each cookbook author must choose how much information to provide so you feel equipped to make a good loaf of bread without becoming overwhelmed in the process.

My aim is to make the journey of baking easy for you. This Bake & Pray method treats the practice as one of spiritual formation—as a process of learning that happens slowly, over time, through continued practice of the same rhythm again and again. In this way, we learn to bake and pray—both through repetition. This learning process is not something that happens in our minds alone, but with our entire bodies.

If you've never made a loaf of bread before, this book is for you.

If you've made many loaves but most of them have failed and you can't figure out why, this book is also for you.

If you are an expert bread baker who masterfully crafts sourdough loaves, the techniques taught in this book might feel basic, but this book is for you too. The simplicity is key to engaging with the process as a method of prayer.

Similarly, if you are intimidated by prayer, if your life feels too busy for prayer, or if you just feel that your prayer practice is a bit stale, this book is for you.

As you learn to bake and to pray, together, you will connect more deeply with God, with God's creation, and with the global and historical communion of saints in a tangible, nourishing way.

THE BAKE & PRAY METHOD

Bread is at once incredibly simple and infinitely complex.

It is, at its core, just four basic ingredients: flour, water, salt, and yeast.

Technically, you could make bread without salt, though it wouldn't taste as good and the texture would be off. You could also make it without yeast. Unleavened bread, anyone? So really, bread could be made with as few as two ingredients.

Yet these ingredients can be mixed and manipulated an infinite number of ways, and new ingredients added, to result in the many different textures and flavors of bread we find around the world. Bakers can commit their entire lives to learning the craft of bread and still find new nuances of flavor and texture every time they bake.

This simultaneous simplicity and complexity is, in many ways, much like the life of faith. The Christian faith can be summed up in the statement "Christ has died, Christ is risen, and Christ will come again." At the same time, we can spend our entire lives drawing closer to God and still learn more about the beauty and character of the Lord.

What I love about this facet of both bread and the life of faith is that we have much to learn in both the simplicity and the complexity.

Some Christians are excited by hours spent wading through dense theological texts. They find joy in translating Scripture from the original Hebrew or Greek, and they see God's beauty in unearthing the writings of theologians past.

Others have never picked up a theological text—many Christians throughout history have never even owned a Bible of their own—but they know God in the rhythms of worship and are familiar with the sound of God's voice.

Likewise, some bakers are invigorated by hours spent studying the makeup of a kernel of wheat. They find joy in tweaking recipes down to a half a degree or tenth of a gram. They are driven by a quest to make the perfect loaf.

Many others—mostly women—have spent their lives making bread on a daily basis just to feed the ones they love. Many have done so without a scale or a thermometer, without reading any books. They know bread and understand its needs through their senses of touch and smell, through lessons passed down from generation to generation.

I will confess: my own shelves are filled with books on theology and books on bread. I could burst with excitement when I encounter new writings that help me see even more of the intricate creativity of God in the chemistry of baking or in the imagery of bread throughout Scripture and Christian tradition.

But over the years, my studies have also taught me to value a simpler, more embodied approach. They've deepened my respect for the bakers who know bread and the Christians who know God through the slow, simple rhythms of their daily lives. This slow, simple, embodied approach does not come as naturally to me, but through it, God has been revealed to me in marvelous ways.

Part 4 of this book, "Recipes for the Church Year," is meant to honor these bakers throughout history and around the world, challenging the perception that a perfect crusty loaf is the true sign of a master baker. In reality, the crusty artisan raised loaf like we will be baking in part 2, "Basics of Bread," is not the daily bread of most humans around the world, as delicious as it might be. Many different baking techniques have been developed around the world based on the heating sources and wheat varieties available in any given region. Flatbreads, fry breads, and soft raised breads have sustained humanity for millennia. Spices, dried fruits, butter, milk, and eggs were incorporated for special occasions, creating an extensive array of bread styles that mark the celebration of holy days. These breads have as rich of a history as the crusty hearth-style loaf—and some might say they are even more delicious.

As you work your way through the methods in this book, I hope that you, too, come to appreciate the slow, simple rhythms of bread and of faith. I hope that you learn to pay attention with all your senses, honing your skills by intuition—striving not for perfection but for joy.

WHY A LITURGY-RECIPE?

Many cookbook writers quip that baking is a science and cooking is an art. Baking requires precision in order to facilitate the right chemical reactions once the dough hits the oven. Cooking, on the other hand, allows for creativity and flexibility—sure, there is some science involved, but an extra clove of garlic or two isn't going to ruin a pot of soup quite like an extra half-teaspoon of baking powder in cookies.

Bread, I would argue, is the exception to this rule.

There are several variables that affect the final loaf of bread. The temperature and humidity of your kitchen, the temperature of your ingredients, and the thirstiness of your flour are the primary three.

It is possible to follow the exact same recipe again and again and wind up with a different loaf each time. The bread I make at my home in North Carolina behaves differently from the loaf I bake at my parents' home in Massachusetts, and both are unique compared to the bread I mixed in a house on the coast of southern California, with the salty breeze blowing through the window. The bread I bake in my home in December is different even from the bread I make in July.

This variability could prove infuriating if your goal as a baker is precision and perfection. But as Bake & Pray bakers, this is not our end. Our aim is to draw closer to God as we dive deeper into the craft of making bread.

For this reason, I prefer to think of bread baking in terms of liturgy rather than recipe.

A liturgy is a rhythm of worship. It is the words and patterns that Christians follow week after week. These rhythms shape the group of worshipers and their perception of God right along with the actual words sung or spoken.

All churches follow a liturgy of some kind, whether formal or informal. For a Catholic, Orthodox, Anglican, or Lutheran church, the liturgy is quite obvious— it includes prayers, genuflections, and signs of the cross that are repeated in every service. For a Southern Baptist or nondenominational church, the liturgy might be less apparent, but it is present nevertheless: usually a time of singing, where worshipers sway or lift their arms, followed by a sermon, and culminating in a benediction or an altar call.

When designed with intention, the liturgy helps guide worshipers into a deeper understanding of God. It serves as the infrastructure for the congregation to invite the Holy Spirit to move. Through the repetition of these words and movements, week after week, worshipers come to understand their meaning more and more—not just in their minds, but with their bodies as well.

The liturgical calendar accomplishes a similar goal. From Advent to Christmas, Lent to Easter, and Pentecost to Ordinary Time, the church calendar rehearses the story of the Christian faith year after year, deepening our understanding of God's ongoing work in the world as we journey through each season.

When we approach bread making similarly—as liturgy rather than recipe— we understand that our task as bakers is to create a set of conditions for us to invite the yeast to do its work. As we repeat the rhythms, bake after bake, we come to understand those conditions more and more. We learn to pay attention to the bread itself and how it responds to the many variables within our own kitchens, and we slowly begin to understand its needs not just with our minds but with our noses and our hands as well.

I hope this process will also shape your approach to your faith life. Faith is not something that can be mastered by reading the right books, speaking the right words, or following the right formula. It is alive and dynamic—it shifts and grows as we deepen in our understanding of the faith tradition we are in and as we draw closer to the God who is behind and before all things.

INGREDIENTS

In keeping with the goal to make bread making as simple and unintimidating as possible, you don't need to spend hundreds of dollars on fancy equipment to get a decent loaf. However, there are some basic ingredients and tools that will help simplify this process.

In the Bake & Pray method, I try to minimize the variables we can control. This allows us to pay attention to the variables we can't control—namely, the temperature and humidity of our kitchen—so we learn how the bread reacts and how we can respond in each bake. Once the basics are mastered, it is much easier to adjust the variables that we do have control over to develop different layers of flavor in our bread.

Flour

We will talk about flour at length in lesson 1, breaking down the different types of flour you might find on the grocery store shelves and how they affect a batch of dough.

All the recipes in this book will work using unbleached, all-purpose flour or bread flour. They have been developed and tested using King Arthur flour—the brand I recommend to all new bakers. King Arthur makes a high-quality flour that is consistent from bag to bag, which is important when attempting to limit as many variables as possible.

You will also need whole-grain flour. I recommend you start with King Arthur whole wheat or with a local grain, if you have the opportunity to support nearby farmers. I often use the sprouted wheat and sprouted spelt from Lindley Mills, a miller located close to me.

If you live outside the United States and King Arthur is difficult to acquire, I recommend choosing a brand of flour that you can purchase consistently. This minimizes the variation from batch to batch as you are learning about the dough and its needs.

Salt

Salt plays an important role in bread. Not only does it elevate the taste of the wheat, it also slows down the yeast and tightens the gluten structure, developing both flavor and texture in the dough.

The recipes in this book are developed using Diamond Crystal kosher salt. A kosher salt is more coarsely ground than average table salt. While table salt often adds a metallic flavor to a dish, thanks to added iodine, kosher salt does a better job elevating the flavors naturally present in food, as salt ought to do. Diamond Crystal kosher salt is evenly ground from box to box, which is helpful for achieving consistency.

While fancier mineral salts, such as pink Himalayan or grey Celtic sea salt, can add flavor and nutrition to the foods you cook, you don't want to use them

A NOTE ON SOURDOUGH

I call the Bake & Pray technique "sourdough on training wheels."

Sourdough baking is a technique that uses a culture of wild yeast and bacteria to leaven the dough. In the United States, the crusty French-style levain method of baking has grown in popularity over the past few decades. While there are many styles of bread leavened with wild yeasts, this is the version most commonly referenced by home bakers as sourdough. It relies on a wet dough and a long fermentation, which allows the culture to slowly transform the dough. These wild yeasts and bacteria can develop incredible flavor and texture in bread, but they are much less predictable than commercial yeast.

Because the Bake & Pray method relies on simplicity and limiting the variables in your dough, I recommend a commercial yeast rather than a wild yeast to leaven your bread, especially if you're just getting started. However, the technique I use—high hydration (a really wet dough) and long fermentation—is very similar to that of a crusty French-style levain. Once you've mastered the techniques in this book, it should be simple to transition into sourdough baking, should you desire. If you'd like to take the step to sourdough bread after building confidence with the Bake & Pray loaf, you'll find similar techniques in Chad Robertson's approach (*Tartine Bread*) and Bryan Ford's approach (*New World Sourdough*).

Many people choose to bake using a sourdough technique because of the purported health benefits, especially for those who are sensitive to gluten or who struggle to digest the starch present in wheat. The long fermentation makes the nutrients in the bread more bioavailable and causes the starches and proteins to digest more easily. Many people with non-Celiac gluten intolerance find that breads made with a long fermentation, such as sourdough, do not affect them the way other baked goods do.

Because the technique used in the Bake & Pray method relies on a long fermentation, it too renders the grain more easily digestible for people with non-Celiac gluten intolerance. While this loaf does not benefit from the added bacterial fermentation of sourdough (our loaf is made using only a yeast fermentation), I have still found that many people who typically struggle to digest bread are able to eat this loaf. However, please consult your doctor or nutritionist before working it into your diet.

If you are experienced in baking with wild yeast and would like to use your sourdough culture for part 2, "Basics of Bread," I recommend following your preferred sourdough bread recipe with these reflections, liturgies, and prayers.

in your baking. These salts do not dissolve evenly, which means they will not get distributed consistently through your dough. Because salt serves a chemical function in addition to developing flavor, this uneven distribution can negatively affect your final loaf.

Yeast

Choosing yeast can be almost as overwhelming as selecting flour. There are so many different kinds, but what is the difference between them all? The two main kinds of yeast available commercially in the United States are instant and active dry.

Both are made up of *Saccharomyces cerevisiae* but are stabilized in different ways. I like to think of it as the difference between a morning person and . . . not a morning person. When instant yeast is mixed into dough, it is awake and ready to go. Active dry yeast, on the other hand, needs some time to get moving—it needs to drink its coffee and read the paper—or, in the case of the yeast, dissolve and eat some sugar. This is why some recipes call for mixing the yeast with water and honey or sugar before adding it to the dry ingredients in a recipe. While active dry yeast can be used in the Bake & Pray method, it is less predictable than instant yeast. Because our goal is to limit as many variables as possible, I recommend using instant yeast. Instant yeast is more stable, so you don't need to worry about whether it has died before you mix up your dough. Instant yeast will keep in the fridge indefinitely, even after being opened.

I use Lesaffre's SAF-instant yeast, either red or gold, which I purchase in one-pound bags and store in a plastic quart-sized container in my fridge. If you're not sure you want to invest in that much yeast quite yet, Fleischmann's RapidRise and Red Star Quick-Rise yeasts are available in smaller quantities.

Tools

The only tools necessary for the Bake & Pray method are a mixing bowl (three-quart size or larger), measuring cups and spoons, plastic wrap or a tea towel, a baking sheet or loaf pan, and pan spray or parchment paper—essentials for any home kitchen. However, there are also a few tools that will make the process easier and improve your final loaf. I've listed them here in the order I would prioritize them.

BOWL SCRAPER (HIGH IMPORTANCE) This tool is the most helpful one to have on hand. Not only does it help you clean out your bowl, clean off your counter, and clean your hands, it also helps you handle the dough more easily. I recommend the Ateco brand.

KITCHEN SCALE (HIGH IMPORTANCE) While you can measure your flour and water by volume with measuring cups, a kitchen scale provides much more precision. You'll notice more consistency in texture from batch to batch when weighing your ingredients. Plus, it's cleaner and simpler than measuring—rather than scooping (and spilling) ingredients, dirtying both a range of measuring cups and your counter, you simply need to pour the ingredients directly into your mixing bowl on the scale. I've provided both weight and volume measurements in every recipe for any ingredient that requires more than one-fourth of a cup, so a scale is not necessary (but it is highly encouraged). I recommend the Escali Primo scale or the Oxo scale with a pull-out display.

FIVE- OR SIX-QUART DUTCH OVEN (MEDIUM IMPORTANCE) While you can make a delicious loaf of bread in a loaf pan or on a baking tray, nothing will give you a beautiful, crisp crust quite like baking in a Dutch oven. I use a Lodge

Dutch oven for my bread—it's cheaper than a Staub or Le Creuset, and it works just as well.

BENCH KNIFE (MEDIUM IMPORTANCE) Like the bowl scraper, a bench knife comes in handy when transferring dough from your counter to your baking vessel, whether that's a baking tray, a loaf pan, or a Dutch oven. It does an even better job than a bowl scraper at cleaning off your counter. It is also useful for dividing your dough if you will be making more than one loaf at a time.

LAME (LOW IMPORTANCE) A lame (pronounced "lahm") is a special razor designed for scoring a loaf of bread. While a lame is fun to use, a sharp paring knife will do just fine—this is what I use when baking at home. If you want to get intricate with your designs, the Wire Monkey UFO lame allows precision and control. The Mure & Peyrot lame is also a baker's favorite.

FOUR-QUART STORAGE TUB (LOW IMPORTANCE) While you can let your dough rest in your mixing bowl, covered with plastic wrap or a damp tea towel, a storage tub can be nice to have on hand. It prevents a crust from forming on top of the dough in a drafty kitchen, and it allows you to stack things on top of your dough if space is tight. The Cambro square or round storage tubs are the baker's classic.

LINEN STORAGE BAG (LOW IMPORTANCE) There are a number of options for storing your bread. I keep mine out in the open on a cutting board, cut side down. I always have a serrated knife on the board alongside softened butter so I can grab a slice whenever I walk by the board. If you want your bread to last more than two days, you might want to store it inside a bag to keep it from going stale. A plastic bag will do just fine, but a linen storage bag is another great low-waste option. The linen also allows the dough to breathe, slowing the staling process while preventing mold that might grow on a loaf stored in a plastic bag. You can find all kinds of beautiful linen bags on Etsy.

The Bake & Pray Master Recipe

ALTHOUGH THIS BOOK TREATS BREAD MAKING AS A LITURGY—
a technique we grow to understand through repetition—rather than a strict formula, we must still have a starting point before we dive into the lessons ahead.

Treat this recipe as just that: a starting point. It will tell you enough to get going, but you will need time and practice with the lessons in the chapters ahead to hone your technique.

I've developed this recipe over several years of teaching this Bake & Pray method. You might notice it has some similarities to Jim Lahey's No-Knead Bread, made famous by Mark Bittman in the *New York Times*. I will gratefully point to the No-Knead method as my original inspiration; however, I've made some adjustments over the years as I've observed what works best for beginner bakers, as well as for the flavor profile most desired by participants in the workshops I teach.

I recommend that you begin by baking this recipe once or twice following only the steps provided here. As you do, make notes in the journaling pages in the back of this book. This will help you remember where you began and learn from your experiences.

3	cups (12.75 ounces) all-purpose or bread flour
1/2	cup (2.3 ounces) whole-wheat flour
1 1/2	teaspoons kosher salt
1/4	teaspoon instant yeast
1 1/2	cups (12 ounces) room-temperature water

1. In a three-quart mixing bowl, mix the flours, salt, and yeast. Add water and mix by hand until fully incorporated into a soft dough. It will feel pretty soupy at first, but this is okay! Cover the bowl with plastic wrap or a damp tea towel and let sit for 30 minutes.

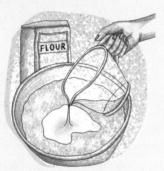

2. After the rest, pick up one side of the dough, stretch it up and fold it in half over the rest of the dough, then rotate the bowl 90 degrees. Repeat this process 4–20 times, until the dough is cohesive and smooth. Cover again and let rest for 8–18 hours. It will more than double in size and loosen up significantly. If you won't be able to bake the dough after this rest period, let it rest at room temperature for just 4 hours and then place it in the refrigerator until you're ready to shape and bake.

 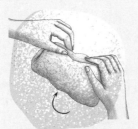  

3. Turn the dough out onto a floured surface, then fold in thirds (like an envelope). Rotate 90 degrees and repeat. Let rest for 10 minutes.

4. Shape the dough by repeating the two envelope folds. Flip the dough seam side down. If baking in a loaf pan or on a baking sheet, prep with pan spray, then transfer the dough to the baking vessel. If baking in a Dutch oven, place the dough on a piece of parchment paper. A bench knife or bowl scraper is helpful when transferring bread from the counter to the baking vessel or parchment paper. Slide the bench knife or bowl scraper under the dough as far as you can, then pick it up, using your free hand to balance any dough that didn't make it onto the surface of the tool. Let dough rest 30–60 minutes, until it has relaxed.

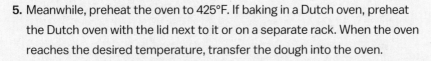

5. Meanwhile, preheat the oven to 425°F. If baking in a Dutch oven, preheat the Dutch oven with the lid next to it or on a separate rack. When the oven reaches the desired temperature, transfer the dough into the oven.

6. Bake for 30–45 minutes. If baking in a Dutch oven, remove the lid halfway through. The bread is finished when the crust has browned and the loaf sounds hollow when tapped.

7. Let the bread rest at room temperature for 30 minutes before serving. Slice and enjoy, preferably with a hearty smear of butter or jam.

PART 2

BASICS

OF BREAD

ON A FALL AFTERNOON IN 2016, I walked to Union Square Donuts with a backpack full of books: my Bible, the *Book of Common Prayer*, and a selection of Peter Reinhart bread-making texts. I settled onto a wooden bench next to the front window with a caramel apple fritter and an iced latte, and I set to work mapping out a workshop on bread making as embodied prayer. I wanted the workshop to be both practical, teaching attendees how to bake bread, and theological, unearthing the spiritual wisdom kneaded through each loaf.

Earlier that year, I'd walked away from a job at a brand-new restaurant, one that was supposed to help put me on the culinary map. I was a rising pastry chef in Boston, and while I loved the invitations to special events, the occasional media coverage, and the creative freedom to craft my own menus, the long hours, intense personalities, and obsessive attention to detail zapped me of the joy that first brought me to that work. On the worst days in that kitchen, when my boss's yelling and my coworkers' crass jokes forced me to question whether I could even make it to the end of my shift, I said Saint Patrick's Breastplate while shaping pita: *Christ before me, Christ behind me, Christ in every eye that sees me,*

I prayed with each turn of the dough. *Christ on every tongue that tastes my food,* I would add.

Then, one day, I'd had enough.

"I quit," I told my chef on a Friday in late April. "Tomorrow is my last shift."

For weeks afterward, I woke up each morning feeling hollow. I didn't know who I was without a job in a high-profile kitchen. I mixed up a loaf of bread each morning, then watched the dough slowly transform over the course of the day. At the time, I didn't have any words to pray. But as in those early-morning bakery hours years before, I sensed God's healing presence as I worked the bread.

By that summer, I was working at a small church plant just outside the city. Simple Church met on Thursday evenings, holding their worship service over the course of a meal. To sustain ourselves financially, and to immerse ourselves in the community, we sold bread at the local farmer's market each week. I'd been hired to develop the bakery further, streamlining its processes and teaching church staff and members to bake alongside me. I hoped the experience would help me rediscover the joy that first drove me to pursue a career in baking and pastry.

"I think you should teach a workshop on bread," Pastor Zach suggested one afternoon while we were shaping cinnamon loaves for the market. "Like how to bake as a form of prayer. It might help people understand why bread is so important to us here."

We scheduled the workshop for the Wednesday before Thanksgiving, and I got to work planning how to structure our time. Eight women and one man attended that first event, each of them excited to bring home a loaf for their family feast the next day. Soon after, I taught the workshop again, this time in my home for a group of friends. Word spread, and by Holy Week, I was teaching the class for the church I attended on Sunday mornings too.

In the years since, I've honed the workshop, streamlining the practical lessons and expanding the spiritual ones as my own theological understanding of bread has deepened. But the basic structure and the themes covered at that original Thanksgiving gathering remain. Over these next six lessons, I will walk you through the same steps I take my workshop attendees through. Better yet, you will have my guidance week after week as you practice each lesson—something I can't do in person with all my attendees!

Every lesson in this book covers a step that can be done with a number of small variations to impact the final loaf. Over time, as you practice these steps and their variations, you will understand the way your dough responds to the unique environment of your kitchen.

Each step of the bread-making process also has something to teach you about the character of God and the life of faith. I encourage you to treat these lessons as a weekly devotional—a reading to further develop your prayer life alongside your baking skills. As you grow in your understanding of daily bread and all that is required to bring it to your table, you will deepen your relationship with the Bread of Life as well.

While it might be tempting to read through all these lessons up front and then attempt to make one perfect loaf, I encourage you to resist that urge. Like the liturgical rhythms of worship, these lessons are best learned by repetition and by slowly layering on new information. Take notes on the journaling pages included in the back of the book with every bake so you can observe what is happening in the bread, as well as what God is doing in you throughout this bread-making journey.

I recommend devoting a full week to each lesson. Take one day to read and reflect on the writing, two days to bake a loaf using the liturgy for the lesson, and another two days to bake a second loaf using the same liturgy once again. If you can't eat two loaves a week, consider giving one away to a neighbor or a friend. Or invite others into your home for a simple dinner of bread, salad, and soup.

LESSON 1:

On Mixing, Flour, and Transformation

MY FINGERS SAT POISED ABOVE THE KEYBOARD, completely still. To my right stood a small plastic container of flour and water that I'd mixed together just a few hours before. It was a sloppy mess. I knew that in the hours and days ahead, the mixture would undergo a massive change, loosening and then bubbling to life. But for the time being, that future felt impossible to wrap my mind around, let alone write about.

It was Ash Wednesday, the start of Lent. I knew that by Easter, my life, like this sourdough starter, would look much different from the way it did that day. The weekend before, I'd been accepted at Duke Divinity School to study the theology of bread. I hadn't told many friends that I'd applied; I hadn't told Simple Church either. It was meant as a safety option, in case funding for my position at the church plant didn't come through, but after a campus visit and a long conversation with the admissions committee, I knew it was the right next step. I was torn between excitement for the opportunity and grief over what I'd have to give up in order to take it.

"Remember, you are flour," I typed into the subject line of my blog.

"I currently have six bags of flour sitting on my shelf: a couple of all-purpose bags, and one each of whole wheat, spelt, semolina, and barley," I continued. "I'd guess a bag of flour doesn't look all that special to most people. It's dry, lifeless. A bag of dust."[1]

After teaching my first bread-making workshop at Simple Church a few months before, I was eager to share more theological reflections on bread with a wider audience. I longed for the chance to study theology formally, but I also loved my job and the opportunities it provided to bake and write. I decided to spend Lent developing a series of baking reflections, teaching people how to make sourdough as a form of prayer throughout the season.

I wanted this Lenten sourdough series to encourage people to start making bread as a prayer practice, but I also hoped that the rhythm of writing would help me process my upcoming move.

I stood up to refill my coffee, the dining chair scraping the wood floor as it slid back. Steaming mug in hand, I leaned against the doorframe and stared into the living and dining rooms. The sun hit just right at this time of morning, washing the two adjoining rooms in a hazy glow. I loved this apartment and the women I'd shared it with for the past three years. Then I looked back at that goopy starter once more. *Change can be good,* I told myself.

I didn't realize on that Ash Wednesday morning that my Lenten sourdough reflections would become an annual endeavor. Over the coming years, the format would change: first a blog, then an email newsletter, then digital communities where I taught live workshops.

Every year, we would begin by mixing our starter on Ash Wednesday, reflecting on our own mortality while rubbing our fingers through lifeless flour. I love watching the dust bubble to life in the first few days of Lent, a foreshadowing of the resurrection we celebrate come Holy Week.

While you are not making sourdough bread with this book and therefore do not need to mix a sourdough starter, the same principles apply when mixing your loaf. On the surface, the first step seems simple. Combine the water, yeast, and flour, and let it rest.

But there is so much going on underneath the surface.

As soon as water touches the wheat, a series of transformations begins. The water floods the grain and begins unraveling two proteins contained inside: glutenin and gliadin. In dry flour, the many strands of glutenin and gliadin are coiled up individually. Once they interact with water, they begin to uncoil and form bonds with each other. Over time, these bonds develop into a network of proteins ready to capture the carbon dioxide released by the yeast, allowing the dough to grow. This protein network, called gluten, functions as the backbone of our dough.

Once the transformation of wheat flour begins, it cannot be reversed. You cannot simply dehydrate the dough, unbond the gluten, and turn it back to flour again. I like to think of this transformation as akin to baptism. Baptism is something mysterious, something we can never fully understand. We are welcomed into the family of God, and in the process, we are transformed. We can never undo what the Holy Spirit has done.

A few years into my Lenten sourdough baking, the significance of mixing flour and water on Ash Wednesday deepened for me. I was guiding a group of bakers as they mixed their flour and water, and I heard myself repeat a line I've said a thousand times: "This flour can never go back to the way it was before."

On the first day of Lent, Christians around the world reflect on the words drawn from Genesis 3:19: "For you are dust and to dust you will return." It's the same verse where bread is introduced in Scripture: "By the sweat of your brow you shall eat bread, until you return to the ground, from which you were taken; for you are dust and to dust you will return."

While we reflect on our own mortality—our own sure death and return to dust—I encourage my Lenten bakers to mix flour and water, substances that feel similar to dirt as it becomes mud. But unlike our inevitable return to soil, this flour, once transformed, can never return to its previous form. This mixture will not turn back to flour but will move on to a new life as bread.

Jesus, like each of us, was formed in the womb of his mother. Fully divine and fully human. But it was not to dust that Jesus returned. In his crucifixion, he offered himself to us as bread—as the body we consume in the Communion feast, which unites us to one another and makes us like him.

From dust we've come, and to dust our bodies will return. But rather than returning to dust, Jesus transformed from body into bread, offering us the hope of eternity too.

After combining the flours, salt, and yeast, form a well in the center of your bowl. Pour the water directly into that well. You'll begin your mix by thickening the water. Pull a small amount of flour into the water and use your hand to rub out any clumps that form. Slowly pull in a little more flour, continuing to rub out clumps until the water is about the texture of a papier-mâché paste. At this point, you can begin pulling in larger volumes of flour until all the flour has been hydrated.

Because wheat's transformation begins as soon as water touches flour, the technique for mixing is important. If we aren't careful, it's possible for dough to form around a pocket of dry flour, which will be nearly impossible to hydrate later. Bringing together two substances of such different textures and viscosities is tricky. Thickening the water with a bit of flour to start makes it easier to incorporate the rest cohesively.

Be careful to use just one hand in this process. If both hands get dirty, it will be hard to clean off the dough, and you will lose a lot of it along the way. In order to keep dough from building up on the working hand, I like to rub it around the edge of the bowl, pulling in the dry flour while using the flour and the friction from the side of the bowl to clean the wet dough from my fingers.

Mix the dough just until all the flour has been hydrated. You don't want pools of dry flour hanging out in the bottom of your bowl, but you don't need the dough to be completely smooth at this point either. If it feels impossible to hydrate all the flour, you might need just a touch more water. As we will discuss in lesson 2, this could be the result of your water being too cold. It could also be the result of living in a dry environment or at a high altitude. It is also possible that, if you're measuring flour by volume rather than weight, you simply have too much flour in your bowl. Add more water just a splash at a time until you are able to hydrate all the flour.

If you have the opposite issue and your dough seems too wet and sticky, leave it alone for the time being. The real test of whether it is too wet will come in about half an hour as you stretch and fold. We will discuss what you are looking for in lesson 3. For now, do the best you can with the sticky dough. If, after you stretch and fold twenty times, it is still impossible to get the dough to hold together, add more flour a tablespoon at a time until the dough is strong enough to hold together.

Once the mix is done, clean as much of the dough as possible from your fingers and add it to the dough in the bowl. (This is where a bowl scraper really comes in handy—it can get almost all the dough off your hands, no matter how sticky.)

Cover the bowl with a damp tea towel and set the dough aside for half an hour. This first short rest is called the autolyse. In this half hour, the enzymes in the flour will begin to transform the texture of the flour, the proteins will start to uncoil, and the dough will undergo its first big change. When you return for the stretch and fold, you will notice that it has transformed from a sticky mass to a strong, cohesive dough.

WHAT TO DO FOR STICKY HANDS

If you have lots of sticky dough on your hands and they feel impossible to clean with a bowl scraper alone, a handy trick is to clean them with flour. Pick up a bit of dry flour and rub your hands together over the trash can. The extra flour will pull the dough off your hands. While this might seem like a waste of flour, it is far better than washing the dough down the sink or cleaning off the dough with kitchen towels.

When dough sticks to your towels or goes through your pipes, it becomes gummy and then dries out and is tough to get off. This will ruin your towels or clog your drain. A little wasted flour is far more economical than discarded kitchen towels or a plumbing bill! Another option is to keep a bowl of warm water in your kitchen sink. You can wash your hands in the bowl and let the dough sink to the bottom. Pour off the water from the top, then pick up the dough in the bottom of the bowl and toss it in the trash. This method works especially well if you are baking with children, who tend to have lots of extra dough to clean off.

In part 1 of this book, I explain briefly the use of all-purpose or bread flour and whole-wheat flour in this recipe. The different types of flour available on the grocery store shelf can be daunting. The biggest difference is the quantity of protein in the flour and the presence or absence of fiber.

Gluten, the protein in flour that serves as the backbone of our loaf, determines the texture of a baked good. A loaf of bread relies on strong gluten formation to rise and create a nice chew. A cake or pie crust, on the other hand, relies on minimal gluten formation to remain tender. Cookies, muffins, and scones need a bit of gluten formation but not a lot. These differences inform which type of flour is best to use.

The section below breaks down the different types of flour available at the store and when you might find them useful.

TYPES OF FLOUR

Sifted Flours

When the fibrous bran and germ are sifted away from flour, the protein and the starch are what remain. A sifted white flour is shelf stable and provides good structure for baked goods.

- **ALL-PURPOSE FLOUR:** a flour typically made from sifted red wheat with 9–11 percent protein. As the name suggests, it's good for a wide variety of purposes—strong enough for bread but tender enough for cookies, muffins, and other baked goods. If you keep only one kind of flour on hand, this should be it. Be sure to buy an unbleached variety, as the proteins in bleached flour are too weak for bread making.

- **BREAD FLOUR:** a flour typically made from sifted hard red wheat with 11–13 percent protein, perfect for bread. If you are going to be making this Bake & Pray recipe regularly, you'll notice better texture with this variety over all-purpose.

- **OO FLOUR:** a finely ground flour made of sifted durum wheat, with lots of strength but not much elasticity; perfect for pasta.

- **CAKE AND PASTRY FLOUR:** a flour typically made from sifted soft red or white wheat with 8–9 percent protein; perfect for tender baked goods such as scones, muffins, pie crusts, and cakes.

Whole-Grain Flours

A whole-grain flour includes the bran and the germ. These nutrients provide a great deal of flavor, but they also shorten the life expectancy of the flour. If you don't bake with whole-grain flours all that often, store them in the refrigerator so they last longer. The fibrous pieces of grain in whole-grain flours soak up lots of water, decrease the ratio of proteins in the flour, and work like scissors, snipping away at the gluten strands we work so hard to achieve. These factors make it difficult for new bakers to bake with 100 percent whole-grain flour. The Bake & Pray loaf includes one-half cup whole-grain flour for flavor and nutrition while maintaining the structure formed through all-purpose or bread flour. You can interchange any of the flours below for the whole-grain flour portion.

- **WHOLE-WHEAT FLOUR:** a flour made from unsifted red or white wheat. Red wheat has a tannic, earthier flavor while white wheat is more mellow.

- **SPELT FLOUR:** a flour made from spelt, a variety of wheat. It functions similarly to red or white wheat but has a nutty flavor without being bitter.

- **BARLEY FLOUR:** a flour with a sweet, malty flavor. Barley bread was the bread of commoners during biblical times.

- **RYE FLOUR:** a flour with a nutty, slightly tangy flavor. It has a higher fiber content than other flours, making for a denser dough that brings out the richness of dark flavors such as chocolate and caramel.

- **SPROUTED-GRAIN FLOUR:** a flour made from germinated and dehydrated grain. The nutrients in sprouted grain are more flavorful and more readily available for the body. I order my sprouted spelt, rye, and wheat from Lindley Mills, which ships nationwide, but you can find sprouted flours at many specialty grocery stores too.

This lesson's liturgy is an invitation to focus on the transformation taking place in the flour as you mix the dough, watching these two very different elements become one. With each loaf, reflect on baptism and God's work of transformation in you. Make notes in the journaling pages in the back of the book to reflect on how your bread develops batch by batch, and what God is doing in you along the way.[1]

---

[1] Turn back to the recipe in part 1 to review the steps in greater detail.

A LITURGY FOR BREAD BAKING,
WITH ATTENTION TO TRANSFORMATION

MISE EN PLACE

Begin by gathering your supplies: 3 cups all-purpose or bread flour and 1/2 cup whole-wheat flour, 1 1/2 teaspoons kosher salt, 1/4 teaspoon instant yeast, 1 1/2 cups room-temperature water, a three-quart mixing bowl, measuring cups and spoons, a bowl scraper, plastic wrap or a tea towel, a baking sheet, loaf pan, or Dutch oven, pan spray or parchment paper, and, if you'd like, your Bible.

As you prepare your workspace, also prepare your heart and mind. Ask God to join you in this process of baking bread. Slowly breathe and meditate on these words:

INHALE: *We are being transformed*
EXHALE: *into God's image.*
2 Corinthians 3:18

MIX

As you measure your ingredients, continue this meditative breathing. Feel the texture and temperature of each element between your fingers as you combine the dry ingredients together. Give thanks for the community of farmers, millers, and grocers who have brought these ingredients to your

kitchen today. Give thanks for the bakers across generations who have passed down these traditions. And give thanks for the Christians who have clung to the closeness of Jesus in the baking and breaking of bread.

When the time comes to mix your dough, inhale and exhale with each line of the following prayer. Pour the water into the center of the well. With your fingers, slowly pull the flour bit by bit into the watery center. Thicken the water slowly, rubbing out dry clumps of flour that form. Contemplate how the substances transform within your hands. Continue mixing until all the flour has been hydrated.

INHALE: *The Word became flesh*
EXHALE: *and dwelt among us.*
INHALE: *From his fullness we have received*
EXHALE: *grace upon grace.*
John 1:14, 16

Cover your mixture with plastic wrap or a damp tea towel and step away to a silent place for half an hour to read, pray, or be still in God's presence. As you do, pray:

> *God, may I trust that transformation takes place, even when my hands and heart are at rest.*

STRETCH AND FOLD

Uncover your mixture once again and grip one side firmly in your hand. Stretch and fold and contemplate the change that has occurred: water flooding and softening the grain, bursting open its tightly wound but untapped strength. Stretch the side and fold it over the dough; rotate the bowl 90 degrees and repeat.

As you build both elasticity and strength, pray in this way:

INHALE: *Oh God (stretch) who comes (fold)*
EXHALE: *to us (stretch) in bread (fold),*
INHALE: *do not (stretch) let us (fold)*
EXHALE: *go (stretch and fold).*

Repeat 4 or more times, as needed, then cover your dough and let it rest for its long fermentation (8–18 hours). If you need to wait more than 18 hours before shaping, let the dough rest for 4 hours, then place it in the fridge until you're ready to bake the loaf.

SHAPE

When your dough is ready for shaping, turn it onto the counter. Marvel at the beauty and strength of your dough, at the bubbles that signal new and growing life. Smell the scent of fermentation, tangy and a little sweet. As you preshape, rest, and shape your dough through a series of envelope folds, pray these words:

God of transformation,
I want to put my trust in you.
I want to rest and believe that you
are at work along the way.

Let this bread in my hands
serve as a constant reminder
that you renew me day by day.

Though doubts may come
and hopes may crumble,
your faithfulness remains the same.
Amen.

When the dough enters its final 30–60 minute proof, relaxing into its new-found strength, repeat these words:

God, just as I step away from this dough, asking the proteins to rest
and the yeast to prove that it is still alive, I ask you to prove your
steadfast love for me.

BAKE

When your loaf is ready for baking, slide it into the preheated oven. Pay attention to the smell that fills your kitchen in the minutes ahead. Find joy in the creativity of God, who made ingredients with the ability to change in this way and who gave humans the idea to combine them.

While the dough bakes, ask the Lord:

Creative God, where are you leading me in the minutes, days, and
months ahead? Equip me for whatever changes are to come.

EAT

After your bread has cooled enough to eat, pick it up, breathe in its scent, and take in its beauty and nourishment. Let a smile form as you thank God for the ability to make something so delicious.

Let your eating be a prayer of its own, a sign of your gratitude to God, as well as God's good gift to you.

On Temperature and Control

I LEANED DOWN TO OPEN THE DOOR to the bottom oven and groaned when I realized it was cold inside. *Not again,* I thought. I turned the knob off and then on again, hoping this time the internal mechanism would catch. On any given day, there was a fifty-fifty chance the bottom oven would decide to cooperate. Sure, every kitchen has its quirks, but a bakery's very existence relies on efficiency in the kitchen, so there are limits to how many quirks an appliance can have before it is replaced.

The kitchen we used at Simple Church was a major shift from all the kitchens I'd baked in before, both in its personality and in its available amenities. For years I'd been taught to treat time like a game of Tetris, never letting a second go to waste. I'd start each morning mapping out the day ahead, fitting quick tasks like packaging granola into the minutes while my dough needed to rest. On summer days when the ovens blazed too hot for the air conditioner to keep up, I'd put ice cubes in my shirt and under the bandana around my head. In the winter, I'd keep the coffee flowing and stand as close to the ovens as possible so my fingers never slowed. I'd work twelve hours straight, sipping coffee and nibbling on pastries as they emerged from the oven so I didn't have to take a break.

The sense of control this routine offered made me feel safe. As a baker, I knew the needs of the dough—its need for slowness, its tendency to respond to the whims of the weather. I was happy to accommodate my day to its needs, aware that in the end I would be able to hold the fruits of my labor.

But I never questioned if I, too, might have needs similar to the dough . . . until I reached the point of total burnout and breakdown.

At Simple Church, no one treated time like a limited resource. The baking itself, not just the bread we sold, was a ministry of the congregation, shaping the members and staff who gathered each week. Congregants who were between jobs came to keep themselves busy, contributing time when they were unable to give to the church financially. Children on summer break came to twist the ties on bread bags and draw customers to our tent at the farmer's market (kids are very effective salespeople!). Nothing about the kitchen was efficient, because efficiency wasn't the point.

It's a good thing efficiency was the least of our concerns, because the space itself was not conducive to it. Instead of belly-height butcher-block tables, a staple in any bakery, we shaped loaves on the same low folding tables that we used for our weekly dinner. We snaked the tables around the kitchen so all the volunteers had a place to stand.

Our ovens were certainly older than I was, possibly even older than my mother. Each one held two full-size sheet trays at a time, but we had to monitor the temperature closely, as the internal thermometer was often wrong. Our sink was prone to clogging, and our utensils had been collected from thrift stores over the years.

At the end of every bake, we packed our things into a closet two rooms over—mixing bowls, ingredients, loaf pans, and all—so other local businesses could use the kitchen while we were gone.

My first week on the job, I convinced the church to purchase a rolling speed rack—a large metal rack that holds sheet trays while they cool—so we didn't have to line the hot trays all along the counter. We also bought a large scale so we didn't have to measure water in mason jars and scoop hundreds of cups of flour. While these additions brought some order to the kitchen, I quickly realized that working in this environment would require me to give up any semblance of control.

The kitchen was hot and humid in the summer and bitingly cold in the winter. To adjust, we mixed our bread with the coldest water available to us when it was hot and the warmest water the yeast could handle when it was cold. More than once, I came in for a shaping shift to find dough oozing over the sides of every container.

While this environment was an adjustment for me, it was a welcome one. The obsessive precision of my previous jobs had worn me thin. The simplicity of this endeavor was humbling but refreshing. In time, I realized true skill was needed to make good bread here. I had to accommodate the variables I could not control, and in this case, there were many. But isn't that how bakers have been making bread for millennia?

I also had to give up the idea that this bread was an expression of me. My name wasn't on the farmer's market sign, as it had been on menus before. Instead, this bread was a communal creation—a gift from the church to the town. Everything about it required my humility.

The flavor and texture of a loaf of bread is formed in response to a wide variety of factors, but none is more impactful than temperature. The temperature of dough, along with the environment the dough is resting in, informs the speed at which the yeast works its way through the dough. When baking with a sourdough culture, which contains a blend of both yeast and bacteria, the temperature also determines the byproducts released during fermentation, impacting the final flavor of the bread.

Many bakers say that the ideal temperature for fermenting bread dough is between 75° and 78°F. This temperature range provides consistent behavior from batch to batch, creating predictability in the resulting bread. However, few of us have the ability to control our kitchen temperature so precisely. Some teachers encourage bakers to purchase heating pads and proofing boxes to control the environment of the dough. But our ancestors have been making bread without thermometers or central heating or electric proofing machines for centuries, which means we, too, can make delicious bread without using expensive equipment to control the environment around us.

Our goal is not perfection or consistent replicability; it is to grow in our understanding of the bread and to view our time spent baking as time spent in the presence of God. To achieve this goal, I encourage you to focus less on what you can calculate with tools and more on what you can observe with your senses.

More important than holding the dough within this three-degree range is understanding how the temperature of the dough (and the environment it's in) impacts the speed of fermentation. Over the course of many bakes, you might also notice how this fermentation time and temperature impacts the resulting texture and flavor.

While we can't control the weather outside or the temperature and humidity of our kitchen, there is one control element we can use to create the best environment for our bread: water.

In a cooler environment, molecules move at a slower pace. As a result, it takes longer for flour to absorb water and for yeast to begin working its way through the dough. This process can be sped up a bit by mixing your dough with warmer water. Conversely, in a warm environment, your flour will absorb water and your yeast will get moving quickly. You can slow the process down by mixing your dough with cooler water.

A longer, cooler fermentation will generally yield more flavorful results, though if you need your bread in a hurry, you might take advantage of a faster, warmer fermentation instead. The temperature of the water is your best tool in manipulating the timing of the dough.

If you're a new baker, I recommend mixing the dough with room-temperature water and observing how your bread behaves. Next time you bake, use slightly cooler or warmer water, depending on the environment you're in, and take notes about the changes in the texture of your dough, as well as the texture and flavor of your final loaf.

You might notice that warmer water leads to a stickier dough, while cooler water results in a dryer dough. This has to do with the way the starches absorb the water. If your dough is so sticky it feels impossible to work with, you probably used water that was a bit too warm. This is not the end of the world—just add a bit more flour until it feels manageable and try using cooler water next time. And if your dough is so dry it's tough to work all the flour in, that's okay! Add a bit more water until you can hydrate all the flour and consider using slightly warmer water next time.

It can be scary to let go of control, as we are doing with this liturgy-recipe. This is one of many reasons bread making has been so good, if challenging, for me. I hope the same is true for you.

The entirety of the Christian faith is an acknowledgment of our lack of control. We are finite creatures, created by God and placed on this earth to tend it. We are interdependent creatures, in need of community to survive and flourish— like our bread, which needs a community of yeasts (and sometimes bacteria). When we spend our lives grasping for control rather than paying attention and responding to the surrounding environment, we set ourselves up for disappointment. But God invites us to release control, to live into the dance of creation, relying on others and allowing others to rely on us. This process is messy at times but also deeply satisfying.

As we get to know God's character more and more, we are able to see the patterns of how God works in our lives, and we are able to trust more and more the ways the Spirit guides us. This ability to let go of control and listen for the movement of the Spirit takes practice, and it sometimes involves a bit of failure. That's okay—this is the only way to grow. And in God, we find endless grace and forgiveness.

When I consider my own penchant for control and my fear of mishearing God's guidance, I turn to a prayer by Trappist monk Thomas Merton. It's called "A Prayer of Unknowing." In it, Merton says, "The fact that I think I am following your will does not mean that I am actually doing so. But I believe that the desire to please you does in fact please you."[2]

God does not ask us to stop trying, stop listening, or remain apathetic while we trust God to move. Rather, God asks us to listen closely and respond as we believe we are being called, all the while trusting God's goodness to meet us in any situation. It takes a lifetime of practice to trust that still, small voice and to respond accordingly. But God is pleased by our desire to listen, and God's grace is bountiful when we stumble or fail.

Similarly, we are not expected to release all control of our bread baking here. But instead of trying to control every element, we are just paying attention to one: the water. It will take practice, and perhaps some failure, to get the temperature and texture just right. It will take understanding with your hands and your whole body, in addition to your brain, to determine how the temperature and humidity affects your dough. But bread, like God, is incredibly forgiving. You'll find so much flexibility as you learn.

This second week of baking, we will pay attention to the environment we are in. We will slow down, breathe deeply, and observe what we feel as we mix our dough. We were created in human bodies. It is only through these bodies that we experience God's creation, and it is through these bodies that we come to understand God as well. For that reason, I encourage you to mix not with a spoon or spatula but by hand.

As you mix, slow down and pay attention to the feel of the flour in your fingers. Pay attention to the water as it touches the wheat. Pay attention to the transformation that takes place in your hands. This process will slow you down and remind you of your embodied nature. It can also serve as a time to thank God for this gift of the body you have.

This slow, tactile process has another benefit. By slowing down and paying attention to your body and the feel of the dough in your fingers every time you bake, you will also be attuned to the differences you feel as the temperature of each element changes from bake to bake.

TEMPERATURE FACTORS

Water Temperature

Learning how to use water to respond to the environment around you can be intimidating at first. It requires time, practice, and close attention to the variations in your loaves. This section is meant to serve as a guide to help you know where to begin and how to troubleshoot issues that might arise. I recommend starting with room-temperature water on your first bake and then noting how the dough behaves. The next time you make bread, you might choose to use water that's a touch warmer or cooler based on your experience with the loaf before.

Desired Dough Temperature

The desired dough temperature, or DDT, is the ideal final temperature after mixing your dough. Bakers use a specific calculation to determine what temperature of water to use to reach this DDT. As Bake & Pray bakers, we don't need to get caught up with this calculation—our goal is to trust our hands to gauge the needs of our dough. But if you are overwhelmed by trying to figure out what temperature range is right for your kitchen, the calculation provides a helpful starting point.

225°F (DDT of 75°F x 3)

- temperature of your kitchen

- temperature of your flour
_____

= Ideal temperature of water

Humidity and Altitude

The humidity of your environment and the altitude you're at will also impact the outcome of your dough. If you are in a very humid environment, you might want to use water that's a few degrees cooler. Alternatively, if you are in a very dry environment, you might want to use water that's a bit warmer. At a high altitude, the air will be dry but the pressure will be low, leading to a faster fermentation. This means you'll need to play around with the water temperature in order to find the sweet spot in your particular kitchen.

FAQS

Q: My dough is really dry after I mixed it up. What should I do?

A: If your dough is very dry, even with weighing your ingredients, it's likely your water was a bit too cool. To adjust for this batch, run your hand under warm water to get it a bit wet, then massage the dough and see if it loosens up. If the dough is so dry you can't incorporate all the flour, add a teaspoon of water at a time until it's wet enough to mix. Let your dough rise in a humid environment, such as in a microwave or an oven with a pot of steaming water next to it. Next time, increase the temperature of your water a few degrees.

Q: My dough is really sticky after I mixed it up. What should I do?

A: If your dough is very sticky, even with weighing your ingredients, it's likely your water was a bit too warm. To adjust for this batch, see if you can build strength during the stretch-and-fold step. If it holds together after twenty to thirty stretches and folds, the dough is good to go. You just might need a bit of extra flour while shaping. If the dough doesn't hold together, add more flour a tablespoon at a time until it's dry enough to mix. Next time, decrease the temperature of your water a few degrees.

Q: My dough is taking forever to rise. What should I do?

A: That's okay! A slow fermentation develops more complex flavors in your dough. If it's moving so slowly it won't be ready when you need it, then move the dough to a warmer spot, such as on top of the refrigerator, in a microwave, or inside a cold oven with a pot of steaming water next to it.

Q: My dough is exploding out of the container after just a few hours. What do I do?

A: First, take a moment to marvel at just how strong your dough is. Did it pop the lid clear across the kitchen? Bread dough is known to do this every now and again. If your dough is moving so quickly that you're worried it will overproof before it has time to develop flavor, then you'll want to cool the dough to slow it down. You likely used water that was a bit too warm for the environment; next time, decrease the water temperature by a few degrees. For now, though, just pop your dough in the fridge until you are ready to bake.

The liturgy included here is designed to help you focus on the ways the elements are impacted by the temperature of water. As you work your way through this liturgy, bear in mind the places you find yourself grasping for control. Ask the Lord to help you release this urge so you can pay better attention to the environment around you.

The first time you bake, use room-temperature water and make notes about the dough in the journaling pages in the back of this book. The second time you bake, use water that is slightly warmer or cooler based on the environment you are currently in. Again, make notes about any shifts you notice in the dough or in yourself.

A LITURGY FOR BREAD BAKING,
WITH ATTENTION TO TEMPERATURE

MISE EN PLACE

Begin by gathering your supplies: 3 cups all-purpose or
bread flour and 1/2 cup whole-wheat flour, 1 1/2 teaspoons kosher salt, 1/4 teaspoon instant yeast, 1 1/2 cups
water (whatever temperature you deem best), a three-
quart mixing bowl, measuring cups and spoons, a bowl
scraper, plastic wrap or a tea towel, a baking sheet, loaf pan,
or Dutch oven, and, if you'd like, your Bible.

As you prepare your workspace, also prepare your heart and mind. Ask God
to join you in this process of baking bread. Slowly breathe and meditate on these
words from Jesus:

INHALE: *Peace I leave with you.*
EXHALE: *My peace I give to you.*
      John 14:27

MIX

As you measure your ingredients, continue this meditative breathing. Feel the texture and temperature of each element between
your fingers as you combine the dry ingredients together. Give
thanks for the community of farmers, millers, and grocers who
have brought these ingredients to your kitchen today. Give
thanks for the bakers across generations who have passed

down these traditions. And give thanks for the Christians who have clung to the closeness of Jesus in the baking and breaking of bread.

When the time comes to mix your dough, inhale and exhale with each line of the following prayer. Pour the water into the center of the well. With your fingers, slowly pull the flour bit by bit into the watery center. Thicken the water slowly, rubbing out dry clumps of flour that form. Contemplate how the substances transform within your hands. Continue mixing until all the flour has been hydrated.

INHALE: *Cast your anxieties on the Lord.*
EXHALE: *Your God cares for you.*
  1 Peter 5:7

Cover your mixture with plastic wrap or a damp tea towel and step away to a silent place for half an hour to read, pray, or be still in God's presence. As you do, pray:

> *God, may I trust that this dough will come to life, even when I release control.*

STRETCH AND FOLD
Uncover your mixture once again and grip one side firmly in your hand. Stretch and fold and contemplate the change that has occurred: water flooding and softening the grain, bursting open its tightly wound but untapped strength. Stretch the side and fold it over the dough; rotate the bowl 90 degrees and repeat.

As you build both elasticity and strength, pray in this way:

INHALE: *Oh God (stretch) who comes (fold)*
EXHALE: *to us (stretch) in bread (fold),*
INHALE: *do not (stretch) let us (fold)*
EXHALE: *go (stretch and fold).*

Repeat 4 or more times, as needed, then cover your dough and let it rest for its long fermentation (8–18 hours). If you need to wait more than 18 hours before shaping, let the dough rest for 4 hours, then place it in the fridge until you're ready to bake the loaf.

SHAPE

When your dough is ready for shaping, turn it onto the counter. Marvel at the beauty and strength of your dough, the bubbles that signal new and growing life. Smell the scent of fermentation, tangy and a little sweet. As you preshape, rest, and shape your dough through a series of envelope folds, pray these words:

> *God of all creation,*
> *you are the author*
> *and perfecter of our faith.*
> *You are forever in control.*
>
> *Help me slow down and*
> *loosen my grip so I might live*
> *in community with those around me:*
>
> *the people, the microbes,*
> *the plants and animals*
> *who rely on me and on whom I rely.*
> *Amen.*

When the dough enters its final 30–60 minute proof, relaxing into its new-found strength, repeat these words:

> *God, just as I step away from this dough, asking the proteins to rest and the yeast to prove that it is still alive, I ask you to prove your faithfulness toward me.*

BAKE

When your loaf is ready for baking, slide it into the preheated oven. Pay attention to the smell that fills your kitchen in the minutes ahead. Find joy in the creativity of God, who made ingredients with the ability to change in this way and who gave humans the idea to combine them.

While the dough bakes, ask the Lord:

> *Creative God, in what areas of my life do I grasp for control? Soften me the way water softens the fibrous compounds in grain so I might put my trust in you.*

EAT

After your bread has cooled enough to eat, pick it up, breathe in its scent, and take in its beauty and nourishment. Let a smile form as you thank God for the ability to make something so delicious.

Let your eating be a prayer of its own, a sign of your gratitude to God, as well as God's good gift to you.

LESSON 3:

On Stretching and Folding

Pastor Zach held the five-pound braided loaf high above his head.

As he repeated Christ's words "This is my body, broken for you," my stomach groaned and my mind raced. Every week I worried whether the loaf had finished baking all the way through. When he tore it open, steam burst from the center. I sighed in relief, and the children gasped and giggled.

After passing pieces around to everyone in the congregation, Zach distributed the rest of the bread to the tables for dinner. The rhythm is meant to connect the bread shared at the Communion table to the bread that we eat at the dinner table. After filling up my plate with salad, mac and cheese, and a bowl of potato soup made with the potatoes and spring onions I'd received from the farmer next door, I found a seat. I chose a table occupied by a couple, their teenage daughter, and their middle school twins; an older couple (Pastor Zach's in-laws); and a single mom with her toddler.

"How is school going?" I asked the older three kids.

"I love my English class!" one of them answered.

"I'm so ready for summer," chimed another.

"We're not!" the mom responded, laughing.

The adults caught up on the past week while the teenager helped the toddler with her meal. The toddler's mom appreciated the support, which allowed her to enjoy much-needed adult conversation.

Once the entire congregation had gone through the buffet line and settled into their chairs, I asked one of the twins if they would read the Scripture for the day before I stood to preach. Three weeks per month, I took the kids to a playroom in the basement during the service. I'd teach them a short Bible lesson while everyone else listened to the sermon and engaged in table discussion. Once a month, though, I stayed upstairs to preach while the associate pastor went down with the kids. This week, I'd also be announcing my forthcoming move.

After my sermon and a round of lively debate around the tables, Pastor Zach told everyone that I had news to share.

"I've loved this year with all of you," I started, trying to hold back tears. "But this summer I'll be moving. I'm going to study theology at Duke Divinity."

A few kids came to give me a hug before I told them we needed to continue with the service, moving our chairs into a big circle for a time of singing. The singing was everyone's favorite part of dinner church. With our bellies full and fresh off good conversations, it was a joy to sing and watch the children dance along to the strum of the guitar.

My work at Simple Church allowed a life rhythm I never could have imagined in my harried restaurant days. I drove out to this Boston suburb three days a week to bake bread, cook soup, and attend the Thursday evening service. The rest of the week I worked from my home kitchen, developing recipes for a small food publication, and on Sundays I attended my home church—an Anglican congregation in Fenway Park.

My Sunday morning church and my Thursday night church were about as opposite as you could get, save the shared practice of eating together as a community. On Sunday mornings, we followed the formal liturgy out of the *Book of Common Prayer*. The priest, deacon, and acolytes processed into the service carrying a cross, with each congregant bowing as the cross passed by. Our Communion liturgy was long, the words carefully chosen and the table purposefully set. The bread, which had been blessed and broken by the priest, was distributed in a manner that ensured no crumbs would touch the floor. Any leftover bread was consumed or returned to the ground outside so the birds and squirrels could eat it. Every detail of the service was designed to guide the community in worship.

After the benediction, the Sunday morning community moved to the fellowship hall to share a big meal where, just like at Simple Church, teenagers and single adults enjoyed playing with the children while their parents got to slow down and relax for a bit. This meal connected the Communion table to the daily table almost as explicitly as the Simple Church meal.

In addition to the differences in worship style, the churches held opposing theological views on all kinds of topics: the role of the pastor, the meaning and purpose of marriage, the function of Scripture, the work of the Holy Spirit.

I'd always loved theology, devouring every book I found on my parents' shelves as early as middle school. One day in high school, I annoyed all my classmates by engaging in a heated debate on predestination with my New Testament teacher. I had a clear sense, even as a teenager, that what we believe and how we live it out matters significantly—and an appreciation for the ways disagreements can lead to fruitful dialogue. My love of theology and commitment to prayerful study helped me navigate the tension between my two different churches. I agreed and disagreed with each of the churches on certain topics. At the same time, I witnessed the gift of living in the tension between two different approaches to the same faith.

Simple Church's structure around the table fostered deep relationships between congregants, many of whom would have never crossed paths outside this service. Some didn't feel comfortable in a traditional Sunday service, others worked shift jobs that required them to work on Sundays, and still others found few other reasons to leave their house.

This living example of the Kingdom of God, built over a meal, expanded my understanding of what God does every time we feast together at the Communion table. It forced me to question what is lost in my formal Sunday rhythm. At the same time, the rich theological tradition that shaped my Sunday service gave me the language to see how God was at work in the Thursday meal. Undergirding both practices of Communion was a recognition that first and foremost, God is the one at work at the Table.

Some might think that participating in such different church communities might suffocate a person's faith. It *was* hard to be constantly confronted with the deep rifts that exist within Christianity, but for me, living in the tension between those differences actually strengthened my faith and fed my love of theological study. In both services, I was reminded, week after week, that God makes us one in the body and blood of Jesus. The bread we share invites us all into the same family of God, no matter how loud we bicker around the table.

After the dough completes its thirty-minute autolyse, it is ready for a series of stretches and folds. This process further interlocks the gluten strands, developing a strong network that provides structure to the dough.

In most bread recipes, kneading does the work of manually or mechanically unraveling the gluten strands and building bonds in the dough. This is why under-kneading can lead to a crumbly loaf and why gluten-free breads are so hard to get right—without sufficient gluten bonds, dough just can't hold together. In a high-hydration and long-fermentation dough like we make with the Bake & Pray technique, water and time do most of the work of unraveling and building gluten bonds. This simple stretch-and-fold is all the dough needs to set it on the right path to keep developing structure during the bulk fermentation—the long rest before the dough is shaped.

Prior to the advent of commercial yeast, bread was most often made with barm—the dregs skimmed off beer as it brewed. These breads require a longer fermentation than commercial yeast. The long fermentation process breaks down the starches naturally present in the wheat, which the yeast feeds on to grow the dough.

With commercial yeast came the ability to speed up the process of making dough. By building gluten strength through kneading and then adding sugar to the dough for the yeast to eat, bakers could shorten the length of fermentation needed, going from dough to bread in a few short hours. While this process might seem long compared to other baked goods made using chemical leaveners such as sodium bicarbonate (baking soda), it is very short in bread-making terms. What bakers have found, though, is that this shortened fermentation from commercial yeasts rapidly diminishes the flavors developed in the bread. It also diminishes the digestibility of a given loaf.

Over the last decade or so, American consumers have increasingly developed adverse reactions to wheat products. For some, the culprit is the autoimmune disorder celiac disease, which causes the body to attack itself in the presence of gluten. For others, the issue is difficulty digesting the starches or gluten—something that can be resolved through a long fermentation.

Think of it like this: wheat is a form of grass. What kinds of animals typically eat grass? Cows. How many stomachs do cows have? Four. As the grass is digested through each stomach, the cow is able to pull out and assimilate more nutrients. As humans, we have just one stomach, and it has a hard time digesting grass. This is why we grind that wheat into flour and turn that flour into bread: these steps do some of the work of breaking down the grain and turning its nutrients into a form more readily available for our bodies. But what the sped-up fermentation of bread has revealed is that, for many of us, further predigestion is necessary. Not only does the long fermentation develop more flavor in the bread, but it also makes the nutrients more readily accessible to our bodies.[3]

Some argue that it's not the fermentation but the rushed harvesting process of American wheat that causes digestive issues. After all, many non-celiac gluten-intolerant people find that they can consume wheat products produced in Europe. In both cases, the vital difference is time. When the bread-making process is slowed down at any phase, from the growth and harvesting of wheat to the fermentation of bread, the bread becomes more acceptable to our bodies. We will examine what this teaches us about rest and the development of flavor in the next lesson, but for now, we will examine its impact on the strength of the loaf.

The two proteins present in wheat, glutenin and gliadin, have two opposing features. Glutenin likes to stretch and stretch. It's what provides an elastic quality to the dough. Gliadin likes to hold its shape, providing what's called a plastic quality to the dough. As these two proteins form bonds with each other, tension builds between them. This tension is what captures the carbon dioxide, allowing the dough to grow while also maintaining its shape.

I don't know about you, but I have always been prone to treat tension as something negative, something to avoid. Tension between disagreeing people or groups, tension between opposing goals—it's something to be resolved as quickly as possible so we can move on with our work, right? But in bread, we see that tension provides necessary strength and structure. It was the value of this tension in bread that helped me notice the value of the tension between my two church communities too.

At the same time, tension needs to be handled with care. And it needs to be managed over a long period of time. In our church communities, in our families, in our friend groups, or online, we would do well to pay attention to this lesson from the bread. Tension will arise, even (perhaps especially) between members of the same faith. Our needs, our experiences, our desires, and our convictions inevitably differ from those around us. Perhaps this diversity is not a weakness, but a strength. It's how God reveals to us our need for one another, and how God shows us our own limitations. This tension can strengthen us and help us grow, but it must be tended carefully in order to build us up rather than break us down.

I like to think of gluten as similar to a toddler. It will do what you want it to do if you let it think this is its own idea. And it needs a lot of naps. When we slowly build up the gluten, gently pushing it in the direction we need it to go, it will begin to work with us—as if that's what it wanted to do all along. And if we pay attention to the gluten, to the moments it's on the verge of a breakdown, and then let it take a rest, we will end up with a really beautiful loaf. But if we fail to tend it carefully, we will have a mess on our hands.

Perhaps this can teach us something about what it means to have a child-like faith.

To stretch and fold the dough, pick up a handful of it on the edge of the bowl. Stretch it up and fold it over the rest of the dough. Rotate the bowl 90 degrees and repeat. You want to stretch it a minimum of four times, but it could take up to twenty times. Stop once the dough either cannot stretch anymore or the dough is cohesive enough to hold together when you stretch and fold.

It is possible that the first couple of stretches will feel messy—rather than stretching, a clump might break off from the original batch. In this case, begin with smaller stretches and folds—you may need to build up some strength slowly. But with each stretch and fold, the dough should come together more.

A dry dough might stretch and fold only four to six times. Still, it should at least be noticeably more malleable than it was before the autolyse. As long as the dough is cohesive and not shaggy, it should be just fine.

A really wet dough might require many stretches and folds to begin holding together. If after twenty stretches it still feels sloppy, go ahead and add a bit more flour—about a tablespoon at a time. When the dough is strong enough to hold together as you stretch it, it's good to go.

Cover the dough with plastic wrap or a damp tea towel, or transfer it to a dough bin, and let it rest for the bulk fermentation.

If you want to flavor your bread with additions such as nuts, seeds, herbs, or cheese, the stretch-and-fold stage is the time to do it. Sprinkle the mix-ins over the dough and then incorporate as you stretch and fold.

The general rule for mix-in amounts is 10 percent by weight. This means that if you are making about 28 ounces of dough, as this recipe does, you will want to use 2 1/2–3 ounces of mix-ins. Bear in mind that this is a general rule, and the actual amount will vary based on the density of your mix-ins. For instance, 3 ounces of rosemary would be a lot of rosemary, whereas 3 ounces of cheese will feel lacking.

SUGGESTED MIX-INS

Spices
For a bolder flavor change, add 1/4–1/2 teaspoon of a spice or spice blend to your flour. You can go for warm spices such as cardamom, cinnamon, or nutmeg or for bold spices such as ginger, coriander, or cumin. I purchase high-quality spices and spice blends from Curio Spice Co., Burlap & Barrel, and Diaspora Co. You can either add spices into the flour before mixing your dough or incorporate them during the stretch and fold for a spice swirl in your dough.

Nuts and Seeds
I love adding walnuts, sesame seeds, flax seeds, and pumpkin seeds to my bread. I stick to the 10 percent rule with these, adding roughly 3 ounces per recipe. You can toast the nuts before adding them or leave them raw.

Dried Fruit
Golden raisins, cherries, cranberries, apricots—the possibilities are endless! To keep your fruit from turning chip-your-tooth hard after baking, soak it in warm juice, tea, or liquor for an hour, then strain well before adding to your dough. I typically increase the amount of dried fruit in my dough, as it is very dense and 10 percent by weight will not get you very far. I soak 5–6 ounces of dried fruit, which I then strain and add to the dough.

Cheese
Whether shredded, grated, or cubed, cheese makes a delicious addition to bread. Shredded or grated cheese will melt into the dough while it bakes, making a more tender crumb. Cubed cheese will create pockets of melted cheese, which is what I love most. As with dried fruit, I increase the amount of cheese in my dough, as 3 ounces just isn't enough for me. I use 4–5 ounces of shredded or grated cheese or 6–7 ounces of cubed cheese.

Other Options
You might consider adding roasted chiles or peppers, olives, herbs, or anything else you can think of. The options are endless! For these additions, the 10 percent rule of thumb is a great place to begin.

Mix and Match
Use two or three of these suggestions for a truly unique dough. Some of my favorites are coriander and golden raisin, rye and sesame seeds, rosemary and kalamata, or poblano and white cheddar.

Once you feel comfortable with the Bake & Pray recipe, there are endless possibilities for mixing up the flavor of your dough.

When adding nuts, seeds, dried fruit, cheese, olives, and more, sprinkle the mix-ins over the dough after the autolyse (that thirty-minute rest right after mixing). Incorporate the mix-ins as you stretch and fold the dough. They'll infuse the dough with flavor during the bulk fermentation. Shape and bake just as you would the plain dough.

As you bake your bread this week, pay attention to the slow development of strength when you stretch and fold the dough. Pay attention throughout the shaping process as well, noting how the gluten builds tension and then relaxes during its rest. Ask God to reveal to you the areas in your life or community where tension can serve to stretch, grow, and strengthen those involved, and ask for wisdom in identifying when that tension needs rest to keep from working against itself. Note in the journaling pages the shifts you see in your bread, as well as the shifts you see in yourself along the way.

A LITURGY FOR BREAD BAKING,
WITH ATTENTION TO STRENGTH

MISE EN PLACE

Begin by gathering your supplies: 3 cups all-purpose or bread flour and 1/2 cup whole-wheat flour, 1 1/2 teaspoons kosher salt, 1/4 teaspoon instant yeast, 1 1/2 cups room-temperature water, a three-quart mixing bowl, measuring cups and spoons, a bowl scraper, plastic wrap or a tea towel, a baking sheet, loaf pan, or Dutch oven, pan spray or parchment paper, and, if you'd like, your Bible.

As you prepare your workspace, also prepare your heart and mind. Ask God to join you in this process of baking bread. Slowly breathe and meditate on these words:

INHALE: *God is our refuge*
EXHALE: *and our strength.*
      Psalm 46:2

MIX

As you measure your ingredients, continue this meditative breathing. Feel the texture and temperature of each element between your fingers as you combine the dry ingredients together. Give thanks for the community of farmers, millers, and grocers who have brought these ingredients to your kitchen today. Give thanks for the bakers across generations who have passed down these traditions. And give thanks for the Christians who have clung to the closeness of Jesus in the baking and breaking of bread.

When the time comes to mix your dough, inhale and exhale with each line of the following prayer. Pour the water into the center of the well. With your fingers, slowly pull the flour bit by bit into the watery center. Thicken the water slowly, rubbing out dry clumps of flour that form. Contemplate how the substances transform within your hands. Continue mixing until all the flour has been hydrated.

INHALE: *My soul is weary with sorrow.*
EXHALE: *Strengthen me according to your Word.*
      Psalm 119:28

Cover your mixture with plastic wrap or a damp tea towel and step away to a silent place for half an hour to read, pray, or be still in God's presence.

As you do, pray:

> *God, may I trust that this dough will build tension and strength when both the dough and I slow down.*

STRETCH AND FOLD

Uncover your mixture once again and grip one side firmly in your hand. Stretch and fold and contemplate the change that has occurred: water flooding and softening the grain, bursting open its tightly wound but untapped strength. Stretch the side and fold it over the dough; rotate the bowl 90 degrees and repeat.

As you build both elasticity and strength, pray in this way:

INHALE: *Oh God (stretch) who comes (fold)*
EXHALE: *to us (stretch) in bread (fold),*
INHALE: *do not (stretch) let us (fold)*
EXHALE: *go (stretch and fold).*

Repeat 4 or more times, as needed, then cover your dough and let it rest for its long fermentation (8–18 hours). If you need to wait more than 18 hours before shaping, let the dough rest for 4 hours, then place it in the fridge until you're ready to bake the loaf.

SHAPE

When your dough is ready for shaping, turn it onto the counter. Marvel at the beauty and strength of your dough, the bubbles that signal new and growing life. Smell the scent of fermentation, tangy and a little sweet. As you preshape, rest, and shape your dough through a series of envelope folds, pray these words:

> *Loving God,*
> *you created humanity*
> *with diverse thoughts*
> *and experiences of the world.*
>
> *We know you more fully*
> *when our opinions rub up against*
> *the convictions of others.*
>
> *Teach us to manage the tension*
> *that builds strength in our community.*
> *Help us find peace in you.*
> *Amen.*

When the dough enters its final 30–60 minute proof, relaxing into its new-found strength, repeat these words:

> *God, just as I step away from this dough, asking the proteins to rest*
> *and the yeast to prove that it is still alive, I ask you to prove your*
> *ability to build strength through tension in me and my community.*

BAKE

When your loaf is ready for baking, slide it into the preheated oven. Pay attention to the smell that fills your kitchen in the minutes ahead. Find joy in the creativity of God, who made ingredients with the ability to change in this way and who gave humans the idea to combine them.

While the dough bakes, ask the Lord:

> *Creative God, where do I run away from tension, and where do I exacerbate it? Slow me like water working its way through the grain so that I might respond to the tension at hand with the wisdom that turns this ache to strength.*

EAT

After your bread has cooled enough to eat, pick it up, breathe in its scent, and take in its beauty and nourishment. Let a smile form as you thank God for the ability to make something so delicious.

Let your eating be a prayer of its own, a sign of your gratitude to God, as well as God's good gift to you.

LESSON 4:

On Timing and Rest

MY MOTHER ARRIVED AT MY NEW HOME IN DURHAM forty-eight hours after I did. I'd found the spot online and had a friend take a look at it before I signed the lease. After weeks of studying all the pictures she sent, I couldn't wait to see the place for myself. By the time Mom arrived, I'd moved in all my boxes and assembled the furniture I'd ordered online. I gave her a tour of the front room, which I was using as a joint living/dining room, through the kitchen, and on to the bedroom. She raised her eyebrows at the bathroom, built inside a former closet and barely big enough to stand in.

"We need to get some liners for these kitchen drawers," she said, her brain immediately processing how to make the place more livable. I had four days until orientation, and I wanted to be fully moved in by then. She wasn't wrong about liners—my utensils had no business touching the old, sticky wood. In addition to the questionable drawers, the vinyl was peeling off the countertops, and I needed baby locks to keep a couple of the cabinet doors closed.

But I couldn't see those details at the time. I was just thrilled to have a kitchen of my own. For three days, we scrubbed and painted and took countless trips to Target, HomeGoods, and local thrift stores. She hung my art, decorated my desk, and arranged my bookshelves. By the time she left, the quirky 1925 duplex felt like home.

As she headed off to the airport, relieved at the state she was leaving me in,

I closed the door behind her and proceeded to the kitchen to make my first loaf of bread in my new home.

My year at Simple Church had offered me the opportunity to practice a new way of relating to bread: as a form of ministry. That season fostered all kinds of theological questions, both personal and professional. Living in the tension between two different church communities left me wanting to understand further how their differences had arisen. And experiencing the ways God spoke and moved through bread fostered a desire to probe further into the role of bread in history and church tradition.

But my new home in Durham gave me something else in relation to bread: the chance to meet God in my personal kitchen, to practice bread making for myself alone and not to sell.

I poured the flour into a bowl—a combination of bread flour and spelt. Since my starter still needed to acclimate to its new home, I used a quarter teaspoon of instant yeast instead. I didn't realize it yet, but I would struggle to keep the starter alive once classes began. This instant yeast would be key to maintaining my rhythm of baking in the years ahead.

Rabbi Abraham Heschel famously said that if you work with your hands, you should sabbath with your mind. And if you work with your mind, you should sabbath with your hands.[4] I'd spent my twenties to this point working with my hands. I was ready for a two-year Sabbath devoted to the life of the mind. Without the physical demands of baking for a large crowd, bread making at home became an invitation to rest. It was this very form of rest that would sustain my studies in the years to come.

The next phase of bread making after the stretch and fold is the bulk fermentation. During the bulk fermentation, the yeasts begin to feast on the starches naturally present in the wheat (or, in recipes with added sugar, on the sugars added to the dough). As the yeasts eat their way through the dough, they release carbon dioxide and ethanol. This gas and alcohol combination leavens and flavors the dough.

Our Bake & Pray recipe relies on a very small amount of yeast, giving it a long time to transform the dough. Because of this small amount of yeast, the recipe also creates a wide margin for the length of fermentation. A recipe with lots of yeast can run the risk of over-fermenting, running out of sugar for the yeast to eat. When this happens, the yeast dies before the dough hits the oven, resulting in a dense, fallen loaf. Without remaining sugar to caramelize in the oven, it also doesn't color or form a nice crust. Given the small amount of yeast present in this dough, it takes much longer to run out of sugar, giving us a flexible margin for the bulk fermentation. In the case of this recipe, you can develop a decent loaf in anywhere between eight and eighteen hours (although I believe the sweet spot is somewhere between twelve and eighteen hours).

This phase of bread making is the most humbling of all.

This phase is responsible for the flavor and texture of our loaf. It's also the phase where we as bakers have the smallest part to play. Our role is to create the proper conditions for our bread. Then we must let it go, trusting that the yeast will do what it is supposed to do.

I don't know about you, but I am terrible at rest. I have so much I want to accomplish, so many tasks I need to get done, that I struggle to slow down. Not only that, but slowing down requires me to still my body and my mind, forcing me to contend with the thoughts and fears I would prefer to push aside.

This is perhaps one of the greatest problems of our technological age: we've developed so many tools and machines to free us from the limits of rest. We have lights that allow us to work all through the night. We have caffeine that can help us stay awake when we're exhausted and Ambien or melatonin that can help us sleep on our own schedule. We have messaging tools that allow us to communicate with friends, family, and coworkers twenty-four hours a day. What all this means is that the work is, quite literally, never finished. We must make an active choice to step away and rest, or our bodies will eventually force us to.

But God invites us—and even commands us—to rest. At the culmination of creation, God set aside time for rest. This was not a time of recovery after the exhausting task of creation but a time to delight in what God had just made. Then God calls us to do the same. In the fourth commandment, we are told to set aside the Sabbath day as holy, to step away from our work. This day of rest is a time to delight in God, in community, and in God's creation.

This rest is humbling. Sometimes it feels impossible. There is so much to do, we simply cannot take a moment off. But this rest reminds us that we are creatures made with natural limitations, and these limits are, in fact, really good.

This rest is not just a reward for accomplishing what we needed to do. It is not just a time of recovery after our work is through. This rest is the time set aside to simply be. And it is through this rest that God transforms and develops and flavors us, just as the yeast transforms and flavors and grows the dough. This change happens slowly, at the microscopic level, but over time we can see the marvelous results. Our long, slow fermentation serves as an ongoing reminder of the formational power of rest—not because of what we accomplish but because of what is accomplished in us.

This rest invites us to trust. We must trust that the yeast will do what the yeast is supposed to do. We must trust that God will do what God promises to do, even if we can't see the results at first. And we must trust that this rest, counterintuitive as it might seem, will actually lead to something far better than if we never took time off at all.

A lack of rest degrades the quality of our loaf. It leaves us with something bland and crumbly, faintly reminiscent of decent bread. If we were to try to work actively with the dough from start to finish, we would end up with a pretty terrible loaf. But by giving the dough a break, and by taking a break ourselves, we receive the delicious gift that comes only through the grace of time.

As we discussed in lesson 2, temperature is one of the most significant variables affecting the length of fermentation in our bread. A dough mixed in the winter will generally move more slowly than one mixed in the heat of summer. A dough mixed with warm water will move more quickly than one mixed with cool water. And a longer fermentation generally provides more time for flavor to develop. If you need to speed up your dough to have it ready in time for dinner, you can mix it with warmer water or store it in a warm place for the bulk fermentation. If you prefer to have the flavors developed by a long, cool fermentation, or if your schedule requires you to stretch out the time between the mix and the bake, you can pop your dough in the refrigerator for an extended fermentation.

You can experiment by making this recipe with different lengths of fermentation. As you do, note the differences from loaf to loaf. The length you choose depends on which texture and flavor is preferable to you—and which works best with your schedule.

I love that this technique is so simple and flexible, making it manageable for the rhythms of our busy lives. Perhaps this is ironic, given the emphasis on rest in this lesson. But I hope this shows you that rest is also something we can fit into our busy lives. In fact, noticing the ways we can prioritize rest will help us better notice the ways rest develops us and equips us in everything else we do.

The chart below is intended to help you think through the timing of your loaf, especially if you are trying to bake between activities, such as work, volunteer commitments, the kids' carpool, or school. If you are baking for a particular occasion, it's helpful to work backward from when you need the finished loaf. But if you simply want to mix and bake as you are able, it will help you think about the role of the refrigerator in the process too.

Bulk Fermentation at Room Temperature

When you keep your dough at room temperature for the entirety of its bulk fermentation, you can rest it anywhere from eight to eighteen hours. The dough might even be good all the way to twenty-four hours, but the environment of your kitchen will impact how long of a fermentation makes the ideal loaf of bread. If your kitchen is chilly, your dough might want a minimum of nine to ten hours to build adequate flavor and strength. If your home is warm, twenty-four hours will definitely take it over the edge. To be safe, I recommend capping your room temperature fermentation at eighteen hours. Within those boundaries, though, you have lots of flexibility.

Combination of Room Temperature and Refrigerated Fermentation

Some bakers prefer to give their dough time in the refrigerator through this bulk fermentation. There are many reasons to refrigerate your dough—by slowing down yeast activity, the refrigerator can extend the length of time you have before baking your dough. This can be handy if you hoped to get to the loaf in the morning before work but you slept through your alarm and need to wait until dinnertime! The colder, slower fermentation also brings out tangier flavors in the bread, which you might prefer. Finally, a cold dough can be easier to shape than a room-temperature dough. If you plan to refrigerate your dough for a portion of the bulk fermentation, you want to make sure to give the yeast plenty of time to wake up at room temperature first. I recommend giving the dough at least four hours at room temperature before popping it into the fridge, though you could give it up to twelve hours. The dough can be held in the refrigerator up to forty-eight hours before baking. Make sure to cover your dough with plastic wrap or place it in a container with a lid—the refrigerator will dry out the top of the dough if it is not covered with something to hold the moisture in.

Refrigerated Finish

If you prefer the flavor and texture of a room-temperature fermented loaf but want the ease of shaping cold dough, you can place the dough in the refrigerator for the final hour of the bulk fermentation before shaping to cool it down, making it less sticky when it's time to turn the dough onto the counter.

Freezing Dough and Freezing Bread

I'm frequently asked if a baker can freeze their dough to have on hand for a fresh loaf at any time. Technically, the answer is yes, you can freeze dough. However, you need to give it twelve hours or more in the refrigerator to defrost before shaping and baking, which means it's not exactly on hand for fresh bread. I don't love the final loaf made with frozen dough either. But a fresh loaf of bread, wrapped tightly, freezes really well. If your goal is to have fresh bread on hand, I recommend freezing loaves as soon as they're cooled. To defrost and return the loaf to its freshest texture, wrap the loaf in aluminum foil and defrost it in a 300°F oven for twenty minutes. Alternatively, you could preslice the bread before freezing it and pull out a piece at a time to pop in the toaster. This is my preferred method.

Experiment with these different times and temperatures until you find a margin that works best for you. You might find that you like the flavor of a long fermentation best or that you like the ease of shaping after a shorter rest. You might prefer the texture of a cold fermentation, as well as the flexibility it provides. Take notes with each loaf to determine which method fits your preferences and schedule.

As you bake your bread this week, pay attention to the transformation that occurs when the dough is at rest. Pay attention, too, to what happens in you when you take the time to slow down. Consider setting aside all your work during the bulk fermentation one day. Does the practice of resting with your dough make you anxious? Hopeful? Does it enable you to truly enjoy the bread you eat on the other side? In your journaling pages, record the differences you notice from loaf to loaf as you rest the dough in different ways. Note also the ways you sense God at work in you as you take the time to slow down.

A LITURGY FOR BREAD BAKING,
WITH ATTENTION TO REST

MISE EN PLACE

Begin by gathering your supplies: 3 cups all-purpose or
bread flour and 1/2 cup whole-wheat flour, 1 1/2 teaspoons kosher salt, 1/4 teaspoon instant yeast, 1 1/2
cups room-temperature water, a three-quart mixing
bowl, measuring cups and spoons, a bowl scraper, plastic
wrap or a tea towel, a baking sheet, loaf pan, or Dutch oven,
pan spray or parchment paper, and, if you'd like, your Bible.

As you prepare your workspace, also prepare your heart and mind. Ask God
to join you in this process of baking bread. Slowly breathe and meditate on these
words from Jesus:

INHALE: *Come to me.*
EXHALE: *I will give you rest.*
Matthew 11:28

MIX

As you measure your ingredients, continue this meditative
breathing. Feel the texture and temperature of each element
between your fingers as you combine the dry ingredients
together. Give thanks for the community of farmers, millers, and grocers who have brought these ingredients to your
kitchen today. Give thanks for the bakers across generations
who have passed down these traditions. And give thanks

for the Christians who have clung to the closeness of Jesus in the baking and breaking of bread.

When the time comes to mix your dough, inhale and exhale with each line of the following prayer. Pour the water into the center of the well. With your fingers, slowly pull the flour bit by bit into the watery center. Thicken the water slowly, rubbing out dry clumps of flour that form. Contemplate how the substances transform within your hands.

INHALE: *My presence will go with you,*
EXHALE: *and I will give you rest.*
       Exodus 33:14

Now stop. The work is not yet done, but it is not all yours to do.

Cover your mixture with a damp towel and step away to a silent place for half an hour to read, pray, or be still in God's presence. As you do, pray:

> *God, may I trust that this dough will be better for these series of rests. May I also trust that I will be blessed by following your commands to slow down.*

STRETCH AND FOLD

Uncover your mixture once again and grip one side firmly in your hand. Stretch and fold and contemplate the change that has occurred: water flooding and softening the grain, bursting open its tightly wound but untapped strength. Stretch the side and fold it over the dough; rotate the bowl 90 degrees and repeat.

As you build both elasticity and strength, pray in this way:

INHALE: *Oh God (stretch) who comes (fold)*
EXHALE: *to us (stretch) in bread (fold),*
INHALE: *do not (stretch) let us (fold)*
EXHALE: *go (stretch and fold).*

Repeat 4 or more times, as needed, then cover your dough and let it rest for its long fermentation (8–18 hours). If you need to wait more than 18 hours before shaping, let the dough in rest for 4 hours, then place it in the fridge until you're ready to bake the loaf.

SHAPE

When your dough is ready for shaping, turn it onto the counter. Marvel at the beauty and strength of your dough, the bubbles that signal new and growing life. Smell the scent of fermentation, tangy and a little sweet. As you preshape, rest, and shape your dough through a series of envelope folds, pray these words:

> *God who rested,*
> *for six days you created*
> *and saw that it was good.*
> *Then on the seventh, you took a break.*
>
> *I struggle to rest,*
> *to slow my body and mind,*
> *to trust that this slowness is good.*
>
> *Teach me to delight*
> *in the boundaries you give:*
> *the call to rest, trust, and enjoy your creation.*
> *Amen.*

When the dough enters its final 30–60 minute proof, relaxing into its new-found strength, repeat these words:

> *God, just as I slow down and take a break, asking the proteins to*
> *rest and the yeast to prove that it is still alive, I ask you to prove your*
> *commitment to caring for me as I offer my labor back to you.*

BAKE

When your loaf is ready for baking, slide it into the preheated oven. Pay attention to the smell that fills your kitchen in the minutes ahead. Find joy in the creativity of God, who made ingredients with the ability to change in this way and who gave humans the idea to combine them.

While the dough bakes, ask the Lord:

> *Loving God, in what areas of my life do I struggle to believe that rest is good? Open my eyes to the times I would prefer to rush ahead when sitting in the process is the proper posture. In these moments, remind me of this dough, made better as it sits still.*

EAT

After your bread has cooled enough to eat, pick it up, breathe in its scent, and take in its beauty and nourishment. Let a smile form as you thank God for the ability to make something so delicious.

Let your eating be a prayer of its own, a sign of your gratitude to God, as well as God's good gift to you.

LESSON 5:

On Shaping

I LAY IN BED AND STARED AT THE CEILING, my dog, Strudel, snoring by my feet. It was just past midnight on the night of my twenty-eighth birthday, and I had an idea. I turned the thought over in my mind a few times before finally turning on my lamp and grabbing some paper and a pencil. I needed to crunch the numbers.

I had one semester left in divinity school, and I wasn't exactly sure what I would do next. I missed baking, but my years at Simple Church and my time studying theology clarified for me that I could not go back to the long hours I'd worked before. I considered going full time as a freelance writer, hoping I could find some gigs developing recipes, but I worried the precarity of that path would be too stressful for me. I wanted to both write and bake, to create a life that balanced physical labor and mental work and that, most importantly, prioritized rest. That night as I lay in bed, reflecting on the year past and praying about the year to come, the idea struck me.

I would start a bread subscription.

I would bake once a week and then deliver the loaves to local churches, which could serve as pickup sites. As thanks for allowing people to pick up loaves there, I would make the churches' weekly Communion loaves. The rhythm would, quite literally, connect the bread shared at the Communion table to the bread consumed throughout the week.

My hand moved furiously as I wrote out the idea. One hundred loaves a week would cover my basic expenses, which I could bake in a two-day stretch. That would leave me the rest of the week to write without the pressure of paying my bills through writing alone. Mentally, physically, and financially, the plan was perfect. "Companion Bread Share," I wrote across the top of the scrap piece of paper.

I sent an email to the owner of the popsicle shop down the road, asking if I could take her to lunch. I'd developed recipes for her the summer before to help her shop expand their offerings of sweets—cookies that maintained some chew when frozen, perfect for ice cream sandwiches, and an assortment of pies. My favorite was strawberry sumac with a lemon cornmeal crust. I wanted to see if the owner would let me use her kitchen in exchange for more recipe development, and I hoped to glean any advice she had on starting a venture of my own.

A few months later, in the fall of 2019, I carried a stack of plastic bins and two massive bags of flour into the popsicle shop for my first bake. I'd run a trial subscription out of my home kitchen during the final semester of school, waking up early to bake as the sun rose in my kitchen window. But there was something about being back in a commercial kitchen that made me feel alive. I flipped on the lights and then the oven, closing my eyes to listen to the muted roar of the exhaust fans. It felt like coming home.

As I mixed that first batch of dough, I reflected on how far I'd come. I thought back to the mornings at Sofra Bakery, praying with each movement, though I was too exhausted to carry on that rhythm much longer. I mentally rushed past the next restaurant endeavor, the one where I prayed Saint Patrick's breastplate while shaping pita to help me ignore the crass jokes and angry yelling all around me. I smiled as I considered the Simple Church kitchen, grateful for the community of church bakers who reshaped my vision for what this work could be.

The journey to this place had been circuitous, but I could see the thread God wove through it all. God guided me through each step of the way, providing time to rest and recover whenever I wore myself thin. *Finally*, I thought. *It's all been leading to this.*

I wheeled the first set of loaves into the walk-in cooler, washed the dishes, and turned out the lights. I'd come back in the morning to bake the bread before delivery. I smiled again as I climbed into my car to leave.

I love this life, I thought as I drove away.

Once the dough has finished its bulk fermentation, it is ready to move into shaping. At this point, the dough has developed just about all its flavor. Now it's the baker's job to build tension across the surface of the loaf so the dough can hold its shape when it goes into the oven.

As I mentioned in lesson 3, tension is vital to our bread. It is in the tension formed between the two opposing qualities of glutenin and gliadin—the elastic and plastic qualities—that carbon dioxide gas is trapped to grow the dough while holding its shape. This tension is vital, yet it must also be handled with care. When the gluten gets weary, we must give it a rest, or we will have a total breakdown on our hands. The shaping process, then, involves a series of moves similar to our stretches and folds in order to build strength, interspersed with rest to let it relax.

This process is similar to building strength in our muscles. If we were to work out every day without giving our bodies time to recover, we'd soon be working against ourselves. It's not the weightlifting on its own that builds strength in our muscles but the time of recovery afterward. Without rest, our muscles would begin to resist us, ultimately leading to injury.

Though this lesson is not about rest, you will see that rest permeates every step of bread making. Rest is vital to shaping our dough. And through rest, God shapes us too.

If at any point the dough begins to resist you or frustrate you or create a big mess in your hands, step away. Let it rest, and take some time to rest yourself too. After both you and the dough take a few deep breaths and let your muscles and your mind relax, you can return to the dough. You're sure to find it a more manageable partner, and your own emotions will be eased for the better too.

When you turn your dough out of the container onto the counter, it will appear pretty slack. The dough will ooze out, relaxing as it spreads. At the same time, this dough is remarkably strong. When I ran my bakery, Companion Bread Share, I stored my dough in bins containing about twenty-five pounds of dough each. I'd stack these bins three high and then leave them for an overnight fermentation. When I came back the next morning, the dough would have grown so much and become so strong that the dough on the bottom could lift the bins on top of it—the lid on the bottom hovering half an inch above the container, held up entirely by dough.

The dough will also appear very sticky. But while it might stick to your hands or your counter a bit, it really would prefer to stick to itself. The dough gets a serious case of FOMO—fear of missing out. It wants to stay attached to the full dough party. But once it begins to stick to your fingers or the counter, the rest of the dough gets confused. Which party does it want to be a part of? The party on your hands? The party on your counter? The party in the big batch of dough? As long as you clean your hands and counter of any bits of dough that stick, the dough should remain content to stick to itself. This is where the bowl scraper comes in handy. Use it to shape your dough, and you'll prevent it from sticking to either your hands or the counter.

If your dough is so sticky that you can't possibly handle it, even with your bowl scraper, you can sprinkle a small bit of flour onto the counter before turning out your dough. This flour will help form a skin on the bottom of the dough that will make it easier for you to manipulate. Be careful not to use too much flour at this point, though. Too much flour will prevent your dough from creating friction against the counter. This friction is important for developing tension across the surface of your dough. Without it, the dough will just slide around on the counter. Excess flour will also keep the dough from sticking to itself, which makes shaping difficult.

Once you've turned your dough onto the counter, the next step is called the preshape. This process is similar to the stretches and folds you did in lesson 3.

Pick up the side of the dough parallel to your body, farthest away, and fold it down one-third of the way. Next, pick up the dough parallel to your body, closest to you, and fold it up one-third of the way. At this point, your dough should be folded as if you are folding a piece of paper to put in an envelope.

Now repeat the same fold from side to side: pick up the right side of the dough and fold it over one-third of the way, then pick up the left side and fold it over one-third of the way. Your dough can stretch farther than you might expect, so don't be afraid to pull it up a bit before folding it over. If the dough is feeling very sticky, try using your bowl scraper instead of your hands to pick it up.

After you've completed the envelope fold both vertically and horizontally, your dough is tired. It needs another nap—about fifteen minutes this time. If your dough has been sticky to work with, consider flipping it over so the seam is on the bottom and then sprinkle the top with a bit of flour and rub it in. During the rest, the dough will form a bit more of a skin on top that will make it easier to perform the final shape.

As the dough rests, it should begin to relax into itself again. It will ooze out, though not as much as it did when you first turned it onto the counter. The dough is ready for its final shape when you can poke it gently and the indentation slowly fills in on itself. If you flipped your dough seam-side down for the rest, flip it over again so the seam faces up—this is the belly of your dough. It will remain sticky and less smooth than the outer skin. This is okay! It will be folded into the center of the loaf, so you won't see it in the end.

The final shape once again looks very similar to the step just before. Begin with your two envelope folds—top to bottom, bottom to top, right to left, left to right. Next, pick up the edge of the dough farthest from you and fold the dough in half so the top edge meets the bottom edge. You should have an oval shaped loaf, with the smooth skin encasing the outside of the dough.

The final step in your shaping process is to create a bit more tension across the top of the dough. To do this, pick up your bowl scraper or bench knife. Place the straight edge against the outer edge of the dough, parallel to your body. Pull the loaf toward your belly. As you do so, imagine that the top of the loaf remains on top. As you pull, you are tucking both the far side and the near side under the dough to create tension across the surface of the loaf.

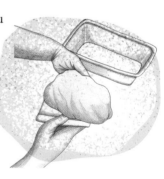

At this point, your next steps will depend on the way you plan to bake your dough. We will discuss the different kinds of baking vessels at length in the next lesson, but for now you can practice with whatever vessel or shape you are most comfortable with.

If you are baking in a loaf pan, your dough is ready at this point. Simply pick up the oval log and drop it in the pan (I recommend spraying the pan with pan spray before placing the dough inside).

If you are baking on a baking sheet or in a Dutch oven, take one extra step to turn your dough into a round loaf. Rotate the dough 90 degrees so the log is facing perpendicular to your body. Place the bowl scraper or bench knife along the far edge like you did before, and pull it toward you once again. At this point, your dough should be closer to a square. Now rotate 45 degrees and repeat with

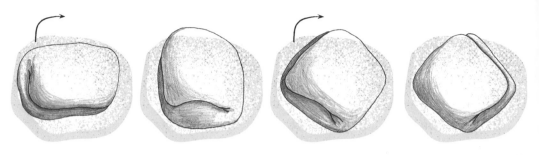

a smaller pull. Rotate again and repeat—just enough to round out the corners, until you have a rounded loaf.

If you are baking on a baking sheet, place the dough directly on the sheet for its final rest. You can use parchment paper or a silicone baking mat underneath if you'd like a nonstick barrier between the dough and the pan.

If you are baking in a Dutch oven, let your shaped loaf rest on the counter while the Dutch oven preheats. You can also rest the dough on a square of parchment paper, if you are more comfortable lowering the parchment paper into the Dutch oven instead of dropping your dough directly into the hot pan.

The final step before your dough goes into the oven is one more rest. Yes, this is yet another time for the dough to relax and for you to breathe as well. During this final rest, we are allowing the gluten to relax completely. Once the dough goes into the oven, the water will immediately turn to steam. As that steam builds pressure, it will force its way outside the dough. In the best circumstances, the pressure will cause the dough to rise into a nice full loaf. If the gluten is tired, though, it will resist the steam and keep it inside. When this happens, the crust will bake too quickly. Once the crust has baked, the steam won't have any method of escape. If you've ever made a loaf of bread that is burned on the outside but still gummy inside, this is most likely why. The gluten was too tired when the dough went into the oven, and no length of baking will allow that water to escape.

The signs that your dough is ready for the oven are the same signs that indicated your dough was ready for its final shape: the tension along the edges will have relaxed, allowing the dough to ooze to the sides just a bit. When you gently poke the dough, the indent will slowly fill in about halfway. This final rest should take about half an hour—just enough time for the oven to thoroughly preheat.

One other option for this dough is to shape it into a braid. Typically, lean doughs like this (without added butter and eggs) are not used for braiding, as they are more slack than enriched doughs. However, I love braiding this dough when making it for Communion. It's messier and requires a bit more finesse than braiding an enriched dough, but the result is worth it.

When braiding the dough, start by dividing it into three or four rectangular pieces rather than preshaping into a round. Dip each piece in flour, then roll into a long, thin rope, like a snake. After the snakes relax for five to ten minutes, shape them into the type of braid you want to make. The following chart shows the steps for shaping a four-strand circular braid.

WAYS OF SHAPING

Preshape for a Sandwich Loaf or Round Loaf

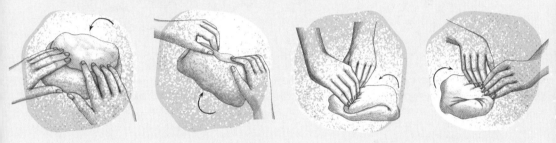

Final Shape for a Sandwich Loaf

Repeat the steps in the preshape before continuing with these steps.

Final Shape for a Round Loaf

Repeat the steps for shaping a sandwich loaf, then rotate the dough 90 degrees and pull taut to form a square. Rotate the square 45 degrees, and gently pull to round out the corner, repeating until you have a round loaf.

Four-Strand Braid

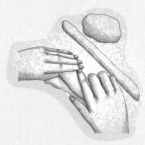 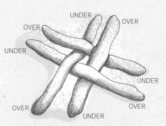 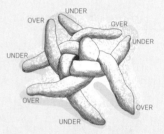

Divide the dough into four equal pieces and preshape by dipping in flour and rolling into a long rope. Let rest for 5–10 minutes before moving on.

Interlock the four strands as shown.

Tuck the four left strands under the parallel right strands to complete your first round of braiding.

Next, pull the four left strands over the strands now immediately to their right.

Repeat the motion, weaving the strands under and over each other until you reach the ends. Tuck the ends under the edges of the round to complete.

As you shape your dough, your job is to pay attention to the dough's response. If it resists you, let it rest. It's letting you know it's tired. While you must nudge the dough in the direction it needs to go, you must also pay attention to the feedback it's providing. I like to think of this process as communicating something about the ways God works in our own lives.

It is difficult to comprehend how our own agency and God's provision and human freedom fit together, especially in a broken world. Learning to listen to the dough in my hands has helped me begin to make sense of this relationship between them. Our bread has a will of its own. It tells us when it needs to rest, what shape it wants to take. It responds to the whims of the weather, behaving differently when it's warm or cold. As bakers, we must learn to tenderly guide it in the way we want it to go, aware of its calling each step of the way: first a snake, then a braid, now a wreath and ready for baking. We respond to its pleas and then shift our plans when it begins to go in a different direction, sometimes guiding it back into place and other times following its lead.

As I twist and braid loaves together, I envision God as a tender baker, kneading, strengthening, and shaping me. I can't see the various forms I'll take in the stages ahead, but I can ask for rest and let God know the direction I desire even as God gently nudges me in the way I need to go.

Over the coming week, as you shape your dough, pay attention to the ways you've watched God slowly nudge and direct and strengthen you.

As you bake through this week's lesson, consider how God has directed you throughout your life. Have there been times when you felt God form you the way a baker forms dough? Do you relax into God's loving hands or resist like tired gluten, weary from all that is being asked of you? Take some time to question how these moments—exhausting as they might be—have also strengthened you.

In the journaling pages, record the behavior of the dough in shaping and make note of the ways God might be directing, strengthening, and forming you in this season.

A LITURGY FOR BREAD BAKING,
WITH ATTENTION TO SPIRITUAL FORMATION

MISE EN PLACE

Begin by gathering your supplies: 3 cups all-purpose or bread flour and 1/2 cup whole-wheat flour, 1 1/2 teaspoons kosher salt, 1/4 teaspoon instant yeast, 1 1/2 cups room-temperature water, a three-quart mixing bowl, measuring cups and spoons, a bowl scraper, plastic wrap or a tea towel, a baking sheet, loaf pan, or Dutch oven, pan spray or parchment paper, and, if you'd like, your Bible.

As you prepare your workspace, also prepare your heart and mind. Ask God to join you in this process of baking bread. Slowly breathe and meditate on these words:

INHALE: *Make me to know your ways, O Lord.*
EXHALE: *Teach me your paths.*
      Psalm 25:4

MIX

As you measure your ingredients, continue this meditative breathing. Feel the texture and temperature of each element between your fingers as you combine the dry ingredients together. Give thanks for the community of farmers, millers, and grocers who have brought these ingredients to your kitchen today. Give thanks for the bakers across generations who have passed down these traditions. And give thanks for the Christians who have clung to the closeness of Jesus in the baking and breaking of bread.

When the time comes to mix your dough, inhale and exhale with each line of the following prayer. Pour the water into the center of the well. With your fingers, slowly pull the flour bit by bit into the watery center. Thicken the water slowly, rubbing out dry clumps of flour that form. Contemplate on how the substances transform within your hands. Continue mixing until all the flour has been hydrated.

INHALE: *The Lord will guide you continually;*
EXHALE: *you shall be like a watered garden.*
   Isaiah 58:11

Cover your mixture with plastic wrap or a damp tea towel and step away to a silent place for half an hour to read, pray, or be still in God's presence. As you do, pray:

> *God, may I trust that I am in your hands, even when I don't feel your presence guiding me. Just as I leave this dough to rest, knowing the amino acids must uncoil, you do not desert me but let me rest in preparation for what's to come.*

STRETCH AND FOLD

Uncover your mixture once again and grip one side firmly in your hand. Stretch and fold and contemplate the change that has occurred: water flooding and softening the grain, bursting open its tightly wound but untapped strength. Stretch the side and fold it over the dough; rotate the bowl 90 degrees and repeat.

As you build both elasticity and strength, pray in this way:

INHALE: *Oh God (stretch) who comes (fold)*
EXHALE: *to us (stretch) in bread (fold),*
INHALE: *do not (stretch) let us (fold)*
EXHALE: *go (stretch and fold).*

Repeat 4 or more times, as needed, then cover your dough and let it rest for its long fermentation (8–18 hours). If you need to wait more than 18 hours before shaping, let the dough rest for 4 hours, then place it in the fridge until you're ready to bake the loaf.

SHAPE

When your dough is ready for shaping, turn it onto the counter. Marvel at the beauty and strength of your dough, the bubbles that signal new and growing life. Smell the scent of fermentation, tangy and a little bit sweet. As you preshape, rest, and shape your dough through a series of envelope folds, pray these words:

Loving God,
you promise to order my steps
and direct my days,
which is both comforting and infuriating.

As I stretch and fold and direct
this dough, soften me to respond
to the guidance of your hands.

Remind me that I, too,
can cry out: I'm tired!
And you will bring rest.
Amen.

When the dough enters its final 30–60 minute proof, relaxing into its new-found strength, repeat these words:

> *God, just as I let this dough rest after building up its strength, I ask you to provide the space to rest and live into the strength you've built in me.*

BAKE

When your loaf is ready for baking, slide it into the preheated oven. Pay attention to the smell that fills your kitchen in the minutes ahead. Find joy in the creativity of God, who made ingredients with the ability to change in this way and who gave humans the idea to combine them.

While the dough bakes, ask the Lord:

> *Loving God, in what areas of my life are you directing me right now? Open my eyes to ways you are forming and shaping me. Keep me soft and malleable in your hands, calling me to rest when I'm too tired to go on.*

EAT

After your bread has cooled enough to eat, pick it up, breathe in its scent, and take in its beauty and nourishment. Let a smile form as you thank God for the ability to make something so delicious.

Let your eating be a prayer of its own, a sign of your gratitude to God, as well as God's good gift to you.

LESSON 6:

On Death and New Life

"GOOD EVENING. IT IS SO GOOD TO BE HERE WITH YOU ALL THIS EVENING!" I said, smiling into the camera across from me. To the left of the camera, my computer showed box upon box of faces smiling right back—each person in their own home kitchen with a mixing bowl and a bag of flour. "I can't wait to guide you through the process of baking as a form of prayer."

I ran Companion Bread Share for close to two years, including the test period during my final semester of school. I mixed late on Wednesday nights and returned each Thursday to bake and deliver. When the COVID-19 pandemic hit in spring of 2020, interest in the bread surged. Friends, family, and even strangers across the country purchased loaves for me to donate to local food banks.

For months, I delivered straight to doorsteps all over the city. By the end of the year, though, my body was worn out. Once again, this rhythm designed to build rest into my weekly routine had become all-consuming. I loved it, but it was no longer serving its intended purpose. The transition from in-person church to virtual worship came right when I was ready to partner with congregations for subscription pick-up spots. The constant pivots in safety precautions meant constant pivots in my business plan too. To continue would require me to give even more of my time, physical labor, and mental energy. The baking/writing balance would be impossible to maintain. Then, just before Thanksgiving, I learned that I would be losing access to my commercial kitchen space. At the end of 2020, I decided to close.

I had a two-month financial runway when I dropped off the last of my Christmas orders, and there were a number of bread-related writing projects on my mind. But I especially missed teaching my Bake & Pray workshops in churches and at schools.

"Can you try teaching it online?" a friend asked one day.

"I suppose so," I responded. "Do you think people would want to learn that way?"

The answer, it turned out, was yes.

In fact, the virtual Bake & Pray workshops offered something the in-person version never could: the opportunity to see how various loaves behaved differently all around the world. In a single workshop, we could have a baker in Australia compare loaves to a baker in Hawaii and one in North Carolina. Participants in other time zones stayed up through the night to join the workshops from beginning to end.

When in-person events became manageable again, I found that the virtual teaching had helped me hone my in-person workshop as well. I taught the workshops to undergraduates through campus ministries, to Sunday schools and small groups, to organizational leaders and cohorts of pastors. Sometimes I spread out the workshop over the course of a full day, developing a retreat where bakers rested along with their bread.

When Companion closed, I grieved. I felt like a failure. I questioned if I had misheard God's guidance. I thought I'd found the rhythm that would enable me to make bread in a manner that honored what the bread had taught me about myself, about God, and about the commitments of my faith. Instead, I was confronted with the limitations of my body and my time. It felt like a death.

Death is a heartbreaking reality in a broken world. The death of loved ones and public figures invokes deep grief, but so does the death of dreams and businesses. As Christians, we believe that death is never the end. We believe in a God who overcame death on the cross and opened for us the promise of resurrection, of new life. We witness small examples of resurrection throughout creation: in the decomposition of food waste into compost that allows seeds to sprout new life. In the forest fires that clear overgrowth, release nutrients into soil, and allow new plants to grow. In the beloved business that closes and allows people around the world to bake as a form of prayer.

While I still have days when I miss the energy of a commercial kitchen, the rhythmic shaping of a hundred loaves, the joy on customers' faces as I drop off bins of warm bread, my body is grateful that I can make a living by mixing just a single loaf of bread and teaching others to do the same.

The workshops born out of the closure of Companion mean the fruits of this method of baking can be multiplied exponentially. It is no longer just I who meets God in the silence of the kitchen. Every workshop participant (and now every reader of this book!) gets to seek God's presence with dough in their hands. And it is no longer just my customers here in Durham, North Carolina, who get to taste the fruits of this embodied worship but everyone you break loaves of bread with. Once again, the bread has taught me to open my eyes to God's movement in unexpected places.

Years ago, I stumbled on a TED talk by the famous American bread baker Peter Reinhart.[5] In it, he reflects on the continuous journey of wheat from grass to flour to dough to bread. He describes the series of deaths and resurrections involved in the process of making bread. Grass must die to become flour, which is then brought back to life by yeast as the flour turns to dough. In the baking process, the wheat and yeast once again sacrifice themselves—dying so that this dough might become bread, the staff of life that has fed humanity for generations.

When I listened to him tell of this journey, I couldn't help but see the gospel woven in along the way. As the dough gives up its life to nourish those who hunger, Christ died and offered himself to us as the Bread of Life. What to us might feel like death is perhaps making room for new life to come bursting forth.

The final phase of bread making is, of course, the baking. While this might seem straightforward, there are a number of different ways you can approach this final bake. It's helpful to know the differences between them in order to decide which features are most important to you.

Professional bakers bake their bread in what's called a deck oven. When a high-hydration dough, like our Bake & Pray dough, goes into a really hot oven, all the water turns immediately to steam. A deck oven traps the steam inside, which keeps the crust supple and allows the bread one final growth spurt during the first half of the bake. Once the interior of the bread has begun to bake, the starches gelatinize around the air pockets created during that push. The baker then releases the steam from the deck oven so the exterior of the bread can caramelize.

This is what allows for a big, beautiful, airy loaf and a gorgeous, blistered crust.

The easiest way for a home baker to replicate the function of a deck oven is by using a Dutch oven. When the Dutch oven is preheated, you can drop the dough inside, put the lid on, and trust that the steam will be trapped inside. Fifteen minutes later, you can take the lid off, releasing the steam and allowing the crust to cook too.

But a Dutch oven isn't the only way to make bread. You can make a delicious loaf without spending $60 to $260 on a large piece of equipment (as beautiful as it may be!). You simply need to create some steam.

In this lesson, I will describe all three forms of baking vessels. I recommend that you give several of them a try to see the difference each makes on the final loaf. I usually rotate between all three, depending on what kind of bread I'm trying to make. When I'm hosting guests, I bake in a Dutch oven. For toast, I bake in a loaf pan. And when I'm braiding a loaf for Communion, I bake directly on a baking tray. This keeps the bread from forming such a crispy crust, which would become a problem when the loaf is being torn and distributed in church.

To bake with a Dutch oven, preheat your Dutch oven along with the oven, separating the base and the lid. I usually put the base on the bottom rack and the lid on the top rack. It is harmful for the ceramic coating on the interior of the Dutch oven to reach a high temperature while empty and closed. By preheating the Dutch oven with your oven, you ensure that the Dutch oven reaches the full

425°F. Once it reaches this temperature, the Dutch oven retains heat well, which means you don't have to worry about temperature loss when removing it to drop the dough inside. This is a huge perk of baking with a Dutch oven!

It can be helpful to transfer your dough from the counter to the Dutch oven using a piece of parchment paper. This also makes it easier to remove the loaf when you're finished baking. If you are really comfortable shaping your dough and know you don't have excess flour on the exterior, you can drop it in without parchment paper. Excess flour on the outside of your dough will glue the loaf to the bottom of the pan when the steam releases (ask me how I know).

Bake your bread for fifteen minutes with the lid on. Remove the lid and bake for twenty more minutes, then check every few minutes until it's done. You'll know it's ready when it's a deep golden brown and if you tap on the top, you hear a hollow thump.

Despite the beautiful crust created with a Dutch oven bake, my favorite vessel to use is a trusty old loaf pan—especially if you're just getting started. You don't have to be too fussy about shaping since the pan provides structure for you. The sandwich loaf is also least affected by the presence or absence of steam in the oven, since the sides of the pan trap steam and encourage the dough upward on their own. If you'd like to add a bit of steam in order to achieve a nicer crust, you can just spritz the top with a spray bottle right before putting the dough in the oven. I use a 9x4 aluminum pan.

Finally, you can bake your bread on a regular baking tray, also called a sheet pan or a cookie tray. You can also use a baking stone. When baking on a baking tray, you have two options for developing that final upward momentum of the dough—what we call "oven spring." First, you could preheat the tray or stone with your oven, just like you'd do when baking with a Dutch oven. With this method, you can drop your dough right onto the preheated tray. The immediate heat on the bottom of the dough helps push the dough upward once it hits the oven. If you're nervous about handling the hot tray like this (it can be dangerous—again, ask me how I know!), you can just place your preshaped dough onto a cold baking sheet and let it rest while the oven preheats. Slide the tray into the oven just like you would a tray of cookies, and you're good to go.

You might not get quite as much lift, but I guarantee it will still result in a great loaf of bread. This is how I make each braided loaf of Communion bread.

When baking on a sheet tray, you will want to create steam inside your oven. The easiest way to do that is to place a 9×13-inch pan of water, filled about an inch and a half high, on the bottom rack while your oven preheats. Then bake your bread on the rack just above it. Fifteen minutes into the bake, carefully remove the pan of water from the oven to let the crust brown. Alternatively, you can use a spray bottle to spritz the top of the loaf when you put your bread in and then spray the sides and top of the oven.

Because the Dutch oven retains heat so well, you don't have to worry about heat loss when opening and closing the main oven door. The interior of the Dutch oven will be just fine. When you're using a loaf pan or a baking tray, keep in mind that the act of opening the door and putting the bread inside will drop the oven temperature anywhere from 10° to 25°F. To account for this loss, I recommend preheating your oven to 450°F and then dropping it down to 425°F once your bread is inside.

Scoring the dough is our final step before placing it in the oven. It might appear to serve only a decorative purpose, but scoring also helps with the final structure of our bread.

When water inside the dough turns to steam in the oven, it's going to search for the weakest spot in the dough to escape. Typically, the circumference at the base of the dough is the weakest. If you've ever pulled your bread from the oven with what appeared to be an extra appendage growing out the side, you've seen the results of steam bursting out of the weakest location.

By scoring the bread, we create a spot of weakness in the top of the dough so we can use the force of steam to our advantage. We direct the steam out the top of the loaf, which helps create oven spring. I love this imagery: the dough's greatest weakness becomes its final form of beauty, not unlike God's ability to use our weaknesses for good.

You can score your dough with a regular kitchen knife or with a special tool called a lame (pronounced "lahm"). A lame is essentially a razor blade on a handle of some kind. Some lames give you lots of control over your cuts, allowing for complex designs. Others are designed for light, swift moves. You don't have to own a lame to get great bread, though. In fact, I own three and I still prefer to use my short, sharp serrated knife. What's most important is that your tool is sharp. A dull blade will just hack the surface of your dough.

With one hand, hold your knife parallel to the dough. With the other, gently hold one edge of your dough so you can maintain tension across the surface as you slice. Pull swiftly. Repeat as many times as necessary to slice half an inch deep.

Once you feel comfortable with your slicing, you can try rotating the blade about 45 degrees when you slice. This will cut the dough at an angle instead of straight down, helping to form the "ear" that some bakers aspire to achieve. If you want to get even more creative, look up bread scoring online and see the intricate designs people cut into their dough.

SCORING A BREAD LOAF

Tips for Scoring

- Your score must be deep! You want to cut about half an inch deep, which will seem super deep at first but will allow the dough to grow in the oven.

- Your score should stretch the length of the surface of your dough. Whether you cut a cross, a straight line, a half-moon, or a square, make sure at least one cut stretches all the way across the top of your dough.

- Multiple long, swift movements are better than one deep move. Most people get nervous about cutting their dough, so they try to saw through slowly, getting as deep as they can right from the start. You want to cut the surface of your dough without ruining the beautiful tension you achieved while shaping. This means you need to use a sharp tool and long, swift movements. It's okay if you need to go back over the cut two or three times to get it deep enough.

Scoring Examples

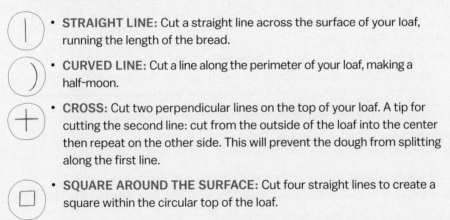

- **STRAIGHT LINE:** Cut a straight line across the surface of your loaf, running the length of the bread.

- **CURVED LINE:** Cut a line along the perimeter of your loaf, making a half-moon.

- **CROSS:** Cut two perpendicular lines on the top of your loaf. A tip for cutting the second line: cut from the outside of the loaf into the center then repeat on the other side. This will prevent the dough from splitting along the first line.

- **SQUARE AROUND THE SURFACE:** Cut four straight lines to create a square within the circular top of the loaf.

- **CURVED LINE ON SANDWICH LOAF:** Cut a curved line along the surface of a sandwich loaf, which will open into a nice ear (the crusty handle that forms on the top of a well-shaped scored loaf).

- **THREE LINES ON SANDWICH LOAF:** Cut three parallel, diagonal lines across the surface of the sandwich loaf.

As you bake your bread this week, consider the ways scoring turns the weakness in the dough into beauty. In the same way, our own weaknesses are made beautiful in Christ. Consider Jesus' death and resurrection: when he was on the cross, Jesus was jeered for being unable to save himself. Like the tempter in the desert, the people yelled at him to save himself if he was truly the Messiah. But in that moment, Jesus knew that while he appeared weak, his true strength—his ability to defeat the power of sin and death—could only be manifested through his death and resurrection.

Reflect on the significance of Christ's sacrifice—giving up his own life that we might have life more abundantly. As you watch the dough transform while it's baking, reflect on the beauty of the resurrection. And as you taste your bread fresh from the oven, remember the bread we receive on Sunday morning—the continued promise that Christ has died, Christ has risen, and Christ will come again.

Take note of your own weaknesses this week, and ask God to help you see how they are being made beautiful. Consider which things that feel like death might in fact be preparing you for resurrection.

A LITURGY FOR BREAD BAKING,
WITH ATTENTION TO WEAKNESSES
BEING MADE INTO BEAUTY

MISE EN PLACE

Begin by gathering your supplies: 3 cups all-purpose or bread flour and 1/2 cup whole-wheat flour, 1 1/2 teaspoons kosher salt, 1/4 teaspoon instant yeast, 1 1/2 cups room-temperature water, a three-quart mixing bowl, measuring cups and spoons, a bowl scraper, plastic wrap or a tea towel, a baking sheet, loaf pan, or Dutch oven, pan spray or parchment paper, and, if you'd like, your Bible.

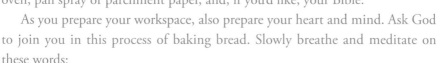

As you prepare your workspace, also prepare your heart and mind. Ask God to join you in this process of baking bread. Slowly breathe and meditate on these words:

INHALE: *My flesh and heart may fail.*
EXHALE: *But God is the strength of my heart.*
       Psalm 73:26

MIX

As you measure your ingredients, continue this meditative breathing. Feel the texture and temperature of each element between your fingers as you combine the dry ingredients together. Give thanks for the community of farmers, millers, and grocers who have brought these ingredients to your kitchen today. Give thanks for the bakers across generations who have passed down these traditions. And give

thanks for the Christians who have clung to the closeness of Jesus in the baking and breaking of bread.

When the time comes to mix your dough, inhale and exhale with each line of the following prayer. Pour the water into the center of the well. With your fingers, slowly pull the flour bit by bit into the watery center. Thicken the water slowly, rubbing out dry clumps of flour that form. Contemplate how the substances transform within your hands. Continue mixing until all the flour has been hydrated.

INHALE: *For when I am weak,*
EXHALE: *then I am strong.*
　　　　2 Corinthians 12:10

Cover your mixture with plastic wrap or a damp tea towel and step away to a silent place for half an hour to read, pray, or be still in God's presence. As you do, pray:

> *God, may I trust that my weaknesses are being made strong. Like this dough that appears so slack, lifeless, and messy, I trust that under the surface, you are at work in me.*

STRETCH AND FOLD

Uncover your mixture once again and grip one side firmly in your hand. Stretch and fold and contemplate the change that has occurred: water flooding and softening the grain, bursting open its tightly wound but untapped strength. Stretch the side and fold it over the dough; rotate the bowl 90 degrees and repeat.

As you build both elasticity and strength, pray in this way:

INHALE: *Oh God (stretch) who comes (fold)*
EXHALE: *to us (stretch) in bread (fold),*
INHALE: *do not (stretch) let us (fold)*
EXHALE: *go (stretch and fold).*

Repeat 4 or more times, as needed, then cover your dough and let it rest for its long fermentation (8–18 hours). If you need to wait more than 18 hours before shaping, let the dough rest for 4 hours, then place it in the fridge until you're ready to bake the loaf.

SHAPE

When your dough is ready for shaping, turn it onto the counter. Marvel at the beauty and strength of your dough, the bubbles that signal new and growing life. Smell the scent of fermentation, tangy and a little sweet. As you preshape, rest, and shape your dough through a series of envelope folds, pray these words:

> *Beautiful God,*
> *you say that all our weaknesses*
> *are made strong in you.*
> *Your power is made perfect in weakness.*
>
> *I do not like the weaknesses*
> *I see within myself—*
> *my body, my anxiety, my strong will.*
>
> *Show me the beauty you are*
> *honing in me, like the energy*
> *channeled through the surface of dough.*
> *Amen.*

When the dough enters its final 30–60 minute proof, relaxing into its new-found strength, repeat these words:

> *God, just as I let this dough settle, preparing for its final score, settle me so that I am prepared to see the beauty you will form out of me.*

BAKE

When your loaf is ready for baking, slide it into the preheated oven. Pay attention to the smell that fills your kitchen in the minutes ahead. Find joy in the creativity of God, who made ingredients with the ability to change in this way and who gave humans the idea to combine them.

While the dough bakes, ask the Lord:

> *Loving God, in what areas of my life are you turning weakness into beauty? Open my eyes to see myself as you see me, a beloved child made in your image, broken yet redeemed.*

EAT

After your bread has cooled enough to eat, pick it up, breathe in its scent, and take in its beauty and nourishment. Let a smile form as you thank God for the ability to make something so delicious.

Let your eating be a prayer of its own, a sign of your gratitude to God, as well as God's good gift to you.

PART 3

A LITURGY FOR
BREAD MAKING

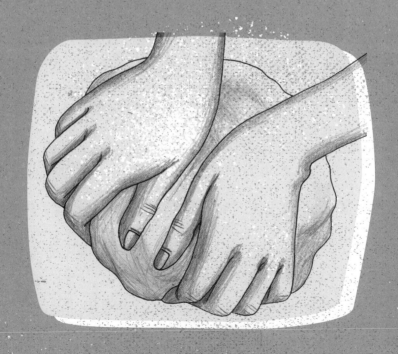

Now that you've learned the basics of bread, as well as the primary ingredients and processes involved, it's time to expand your baking repertoire. The next two parts of this book are designed to help you bake as a spiritual practice throughout the year, using bread as a method of building community with Christians through history and around the world.

These recipes and prayers are designed to parallel the rhythms of a prayer book, following a simple liturgy that can be adapted for each baking occasion by changing out the breath prayers and collects (pronounced "KAH-likts").

A collect is a short, written prayer composed for a particular occasion. Typically, a collect opens by naming a particular attribute of God and then making a petition that relates to the attribute named. Each prayer also includes a line of thanksgiving or praise. The proper collect for a particular date or occasion can be inserted into the Daily Office liturgy—the morning or evening prayer service in the *Book of Common Prayer*.

This book offers a variety of collects and breath prayers for various occasions that can be inserted into the Liturgy for Baking Bread. They are designed to help you turn any occasion for baking into a time of prayer.

You will find a collect and a breath prayer for each liturgical season in part 4, "Recipes for the Church Year." In part 5, "Prayers for Every Occasion," you will find collects for specific circumstances, such as baking for someone who is grieving, baking for someone who is celebrating, or baking for a new neighbor.

All these collects are designed to be used in the Liturgy for Bread Baking that follows. You can consider writing collects of your own for any additional baking occasions that arise. As you might notice, this version of the liturgy is simpler than the liturgy provided in the preceding lessons. It is designed for use with a wide variety of breads beyond just the Bake & Pray loaf—I want you to be able to use it anytime you step into the kitchen to make bread. You will see sections marked for a breath prayer and a collect—these are the places you can insert the prayers provided for the season or the occasion you are baking for, or you can insert prayers of your own.

A LITURGY FOR BREAD BAKING

MISE EN PLACE

Begin by gathering your supplies. As you prepare your workspace, also prepare your heart and mind. Ask God to join you in this process of baking bread. Slowly breathe and meditate on these words:

INHALE: *My soul finds rest*
EXHALE: *in God alone.*
       Psalm 62:1

MIX

As you measure your ingredients, continue this meditative breathing. Feel the texture and temperature of each element between your fingers as you combine the dry ingredients together. Give thanks for the community of farmers, millers, and grocers who have brought these ingredients to your kitchen today. Give thanks for the bakers across generations who have passed down these traditions. And give thanks for the Christians who have clung to the closeness of Jesus in the baking and breaking of bread.

When the time comes to mix your dough, **inhale and exhale with each line of the breath prayer of your choosing**. Contemplate how the substances transform within your hands.

Cover your mixture with plastic wrap or a damp tea towel and step away to a silent place for half an hour to read, pray, or be still in God's presence. As you do, pray:

> *God, may I trust that transformation takes place, even when my hands and heart are at rest.*

SHAPE

When your dough is ready for shaping, turn it onto the counter. Marvel at the beauty and strength of your dough, at the bubbles that signal new and growing life. Smell the scent of fermentation, tangy and a little bit sweet. As you divide, stretch, round, or fold, **pray the words of the collect of your choosing**.

When the dough enters its final proof, relaxing into its newfound strength, repeat these words:

> *God, just as I step away from this dough, asking the proteins to rest and the yeast to prove that it is still alive, I ask you to prove your continual steadfast love for me.*

BAKE

When your loaf is ready for baking, slide it into the preheated oven. If your oven door allows you to see inside, watch the dough rise, burp, then fall into shape. Pay attention to the smell that fills your kitchen in the minutes ahead. Find joy in the creativity of God, who made ingredients with the ability to change in this way and who gave humans the idea to combine them.

While the dough bakes, ask the Lord:

> *Creative God, where are you leading me in the minutes, days, and months ahead? Equip me for whatever changes are to come.*

EAT

After your bread has cooled enough for you to eat, pick it up, breathe in its scent, and take in its beauty and nourishment. Let a smile form as you thank God for the ability to make something so delicious.

Let your eating be a prayer of its own, a sign of your gratitude to God, as well as God's good gift to you.

PART 4

RECIPES FOR THE CHURCH YEAR

THE LITURGICAL CALENDAR is a method of organizing time that tells the story of Jesus again every year. Many churches mark the liturgical seasons with slight changes to the rhythms of their weekly worship—changing the colors of fabrics on the altar, for instance, or changing the words or prayers used during Communion. Whether or not your church marks the changes of the church year, you can embrace its rhythms in your daily life. A simple way to begin is by baking recipes connected to the different seasons and learning how these recipes came about.

The liturgical year opens four weeks before Christmas with the season of Advent. This season is a time of preparation to celebrate the birth of Christ as well as the promise of Christ's return. On December 25, the season shifts to Christmas—a twelve-day celebration of Christ's incarnation. January 6 marks the day the Magi came to visit Jesus, opening the season of Epiphany, which lasts until the beginning of Lent. Lent is a fasting season leading up to Holy Week—a time to reflect on Jesus' earthly ministry. Holy Week marks Jesus' death and resurrection, culminating in Easter, a fifty-day celebration of Jesus' defeat of death. The Eastertide season ends with Pentecost, a celebration of the Holy Spirit's descent on God's people and the beginning of Ordinary Time. Ordinary Time is the longest season of the church year. Despite its name, it is anything but ordinary. Ordinary Time remembers the faithful followers of Jesus who have continued his ministry on earth following his resurrection and ascension. Scattered throughout these seasons are a variety of feast days that mark their lives and their work here on earth.

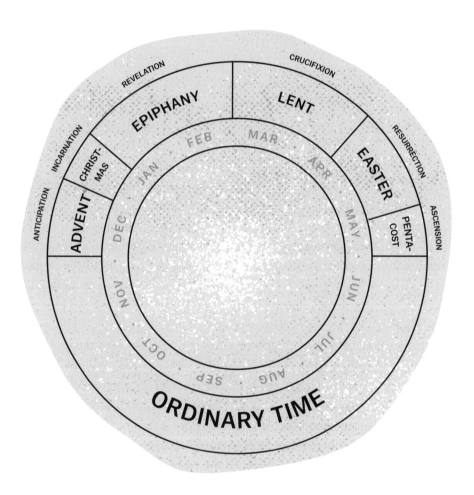

Over the years, as Christianity spread around the world, it was common for folk festivals of various regions to be adopted into the Christian calendar. Many of these festivals fell on days that marked the changing of the seasons, shifts that any pre-industrial society would have paid close attention to. In addition to marking the changing days, the holidays became opportunities to tell stories of the Christian faith, whether stories from the Bible or stories about faithful followers of Jesus in the years since.

As we mark the liturgical calendar year after year, telling these stories of the faith, we grow in our understanding of God's ongoing work in the world. We experience the anticipation of Advent and the ache of waiting for Christ's return, which enables us to more fully celebrate Jesus' incarnation and the promise that he will come again. We allow ourselves to confront the deep brokenness of the world and the harmful patterns of our own lives, which prepares us to feel the full weight of Jesus' death and resurrection. And by honoring those who have come before us, we are reminded that we are a part of a large community of Christians who have sought to reflect God's love in this world and have carried on the faith from generation to generation.

The breads in this section are drawn from the traditions of Christians all around the world, developed through practices unique to different geographic locations as well as to Orthodox, Catholic, or Protestant beliefs. Many of them have roots in pre-Christian folk traditions as well. Some recipes are connected to liturgical seasons such as Epiphany, Lent, or Easter, while others are tied to specific feast days within those seasons, such as Las Posadas or the Feast of Santa Lucia. Each recipe also includes a bit of history behind the treat. As you bake these breads and learn about the many manifestations of Christianity around the world, I hope you quite literally taste the ways we are made one in the Bread.

As you might notice, there are some geographic regions where Christianity thrives that are not represented here. While some form of bread is made in nearly every area of the world, the kind of bread that is common in any given region depends on the types of grains that flourish in that area as well as the common methods of cooking. In many parts of the world, food preparation takes place over a fire or in a pit rather than in an oven. In these regions, fried breads and flatbreads are often prevalent. In order to make loaf breads like the ones in this book, bakers must have access to two things: wheat flour with strong gluten and an oven to bake in. The recipes in this section are all from areas of the world where both elements are common, but they are by no means a comprehensive picture of the breads consumed by Christians around the world on a daily basis.

You might also notice that the techniques in this section are slightly different from those used for the Bake & Pray loaf. While the recipe we learned in part 2, "Basics of Bread," is made with a lean dough, these breads are almost entirely made with enriched doughs, using oil, butter, eggs, or milk to create a tender texture. Many of them include sugar as well as spices, citrus, or dried fruits. Historically, these additions would have been expensive and therefore reserved for holidays or other special occasions. These doughs will not be nearly as slack as the Bake & Pray dough, thanks to the presence of fat, though they might be sticky when you first start to knead them. They will also undergo a shorter fermentation and utilize more yeast. The flavor in these breads comes predominantly from the rich ingredients. Still, the same principles of mixing, resting, and balancing time and temperature all apply.

MEASURING YOUR INGREDIENTS

As with the Bake & Pray loaf, I recommend using weight measurements for your ingredients—or at least for the flour. Weight measurements are much more precise than volume, as the amount of flour packed into your measuring cup can vary significantly. If you don't have a scale, be sure to measure your flour by spooning it into the measuring cup and leveling it with a knife. Don't scoop up the flour directly with your measuring cup, as this will result in too much flour, creating a much denser dough.

KNEADING

Kneading enriched doughs by hand can be tricky. The addition of oil, butter, and/or eggs makes them quite sticky in the beginning. Additionally, as you learned when making the Bake & Pray loaf, the temperature and humidity will significantly affect the texture of your dough. While all these recipes can be made with a stand mixer using the dough hook attachment, they can also all be mixed by hand. Consider attempting each recipe by hand at least once, paying attention to the textures and their transformation as part of your prayerful meditation.

Stretch and Fold

After incorporating all the ingredients, begin kneading with the same movements used when stretching and folding your Bake & Pray dough. Pick up a piece of the dough, stretch it up, and fold it over the rest of the dough. Rotate your bowl and repeat. Once the dough begins to smooth out, you can start kneading the dough inside the bowl.

Kneading in the Bowl

After stretching and folding your dough a few times, you can progress to kneading it inside the bowl. Fold the dough in half and press it with the heel of your hand. Rotate the bowl and repeat. If the dough is sticking to your hands, clean it off with a bowl scraper and continue kneading. If the dough is unmanageably sticky, dip your hands in a bit of flour and continue kneading.

Continue this process until the dough begins to pick up off the sides of the bowl and feels smooth enough to turn out onto the counter. If the dough is very sticky, it might never reach the point where you can knead it on the counter. This is okay! In that case, knead it in the bowl until it passes the windowpane test (see Windowpane Test sidebar).

Kneading on the Counter

If your dough reaches the point where you can manageably knead it on the counter, turn it onto a clean, dry countertop. If your counters aren't conducive to kneading (whether they are tile, scratched up, or simply lacking space), you can purchase a large wooden cutting board to knead on.

Use a similar motion to how you'd knead in the bowl: fold the dough in half, press it with the heel of your hand, rotate the dough, and repeat. The dough might stick to the counter to begin with. If it does, simply use your bowl scraper to clean it up. Then add it back to the rest of the dough and continue kneading.

If the dough remains very sticky, you can add more flour as you knead—about a tablespoon at a time (up to two tablespoons per recipe).

If the dough begins to resist you and you can't continue kneading but it doesn't yet pass the windowpane test, let the dough rest for five to ten minutes and then continue kneading.

KNEADING WITH A STAND MIXER

If the recipe calls for kneading on the counter or in the bowl, the dough can also be kneaded in a stand mixer. Use the dough hook attachment and knead on medium-low speed for eight to ten minutes. Keep an eye on the mixer, as thicker doughs can make the mixer "dance" across the countertop—I've watched more than one mixer dance right off the counter! After two minutes, stop the mixer and clean the sides and bottom of the bowl to make sure all the ingredients have been fully incorporated.

If the recipe calls for adding butter partway through the kneading process, mix the dough for six minutes before adding the butter. Continue mixing until the butter is fully incorporated into the dough.

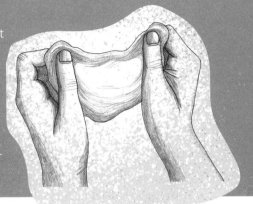

Slap and Fold

Once you're comfortable kneading your dough in the bowl, you might enjoy practicing the slap-and-fold method. This method works well with doughs that are too sticky to knead on the counter. Pick up the dough and slap one end on the counter. Throw the other half over to fold the dough in half. Pick it up and repeat. The dough will begin to cohere into a smooth dough.

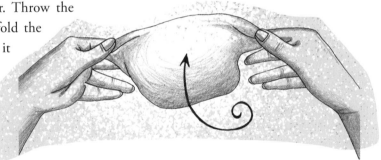

PREPARING YOUR BAKE

Pans

When the recipe calls for a baking sheet, I recommend lining your pan with either parchment paper or a silicone baking mat. This will prevent the dough from sticking and helps prevent the bottom from overbrowning.

The default pan for the recipes in this book is a 13×18-inch baking tray, also known as a half sheet tray.

When the recipe calls for baking in a cake pan or a 9×13-inch pan, prepare the pan by spraying the bottom and sides with pan spray.

Egg Wash

Many of the recipes included in this book call for brushing the dough with an egg wash before putting it in the oven. An egg wash is made by whisking together an egg with a tablespoon of water or milk until smooth. An egg wash made with a single egg will be more than enough for a single recipe.

I store mine in a four-ounce mason jar, always keeping some on hand. If you don't bake often enough to warrant keeping egg wash on hand, you can add the extra egg wash to scrambled eggs.

SPECIAL INGREDIENTS

Some of the ingredients in this section might not be part of your typical pantry rotation. You can find almost all of them online, but here are some other options for where you can look.

- SPICES: I love purchasing spices (especially cardamom, saffron, mahlab, turmeric, nigella seeds, and salts) from Curio Spice Co., Burlap & Barrel, and Diaspora Co. These spice purveyors work directly with spice farmers, ensuring fair pay as well as high-quality spices. Better yet, these companies will provide you with recipe recommendations for your new spices so you can find other creative uses for them after you've made your bread. I assure you, even if you don't think you're much of a spice connoisseur, these vibrant, high-quality spices will completely change your mind.
- RUM: For baking with rum, I recommend using dark rum. The flavor will come through more robustly when using dark rum rather than white. If you don't typically keep liquor in your home, you can purchase a 1.7-ounce nip for about a dollar, which will be just enough for most of the recipes in this book (you'll need four nips for the stollen).

- ALMOND PASTE: The recipes in this book were developed using Solo brand almond paste, although other brands can be used as well. Some mainstream and specialty grocery stores carry almond paste in their baking aisle. I can always find it at one of my local Harris Teeters but not the other! If you can't find it at your grocery store, you can purchase it online or even make your own using blanched almonds, powdered sugar, and egg whites. You can find all sorts of almond paste recipes online.
- BANANA LEAVES: I purchase my banana leaves at my local Hispanic grocery store. They can be found in the produce section for just a couple of dollars. If you can't find enset (false banana) or banana leaves, you can use lettuce leaves or even parchment paper.
- GUAVA PASTE AND DULCE DE LECHE: If your grocery store has a robust Latin or Hispanic section, you will likely find these ingredients there. Otherwise, you can find them at a Hispanic grocery store or online.
- ORANGE BLOSSOM WATER: If your grocery store has a robust Middle Eastern or Eastern Mediterranean section, you will likely find orange blossom water there. Otherwise, you can find it at a Middle Eastern or Indian grocery store. My preferred orange blossom water is Al Wadi. If you'd like to purchase an especially nice variety, the Mymouné brand available through Curio Spice Co. is delicious. If you'd like an idea for how to use leftover orange blossom water, I love putting a capful in my glass of plain sparkling water.
- A NOTE ON MILK: These recipes were developed using whole milk, but you can substitute your favorite low-fat or nondairy milk if preferred.

Advent

THE SEASON OF ADVENT—the four weeks leading up to Christmas—is the start of the liturgical year. It is, historically, a season of penitence and fasting, a stark contrast from the commercialized Christmas season today.

While the Christmas season is focused on Christ's first coming, the Advent season is a time of preparation for that celebration, as well as a time of preparation for Christ's return. The Scripture readings during Advent are meant to remind us of our desperate need for redemption. "The disappointment, brokenness, suffering, and pain that characterize life in this present world is held in dynamic tension with the promise of future glory that is yet to come," writes Fleming Rutledge in her book *Advent*.[1]

This season serves as a reminder that we live between times, between the already and not yet; that Christ has already come, but he has not yet completed the work he came to do. It invites us to look honestly at the groaning of creation, at the aching in our own lives, with certain hope that Christ will come again.

For medieval Christians, this season of fasting demanded abstention from animal products—meat, eggs, milk, and butter. Christians in Orthodox traditions continue to fast during this season, which they call the Nativity Fast, abstaining from meat and dairy products, and on some days, fish, oil, and wine. Because of this fast, the bread consumed during Advent primarily would have been a lean bread like the Bake & Pray loaf.

But all fasting seasons in the Christian calendar contain feast days within them. These feasts within a fast are glimmers of the grace of God, reminders that even as we wait in hope for Christ's return, we still experience the beauty and delight of God's world today. These feasts are a small taste of the New Creation we watch and wait for.

BREATH PRAYER
INHALE: *O come, O come, Emmanuel,*
EXHALE: *and ransom captive Israel.*

COLLECT
Patient God,
as creation groans
and our bodies ache,
we wait for you.

You, who came as infant,
born to young mother in
Bethlehem: the House of Bread.

As we knead this dough,
help us remember:
you will come again.
Amen.

Santa Lucia Buns

Feast of Santa Lucia (December 13) | Difficulty Level: +++ | Makes 20 buns

THE FEAST DAY OF SAINT LUCY falls on December 13, celebrated primarily in Sweden and other Scandinavian countries. The day honors the fourth-century martyr who is said to have worn a crown of candles to illuminate the way as she walked through the catacombs, bringing food to Christians in hiding.

It's said that the Roman authorities threatened to force Lucy into prostitution for refusing to renounce her faith, but when they came to take her, she couldn't be moved. Next they tried to burn her, but her body resisted the flames. Finally, they stabbed her in the throat so she could no longer proclaim her faith, but she continued to live. Finally, she was allowed to receive her last rites and went peacefully to meet her Maker.

To honor Saint Lucy's faithfulness, one girl in each family dresses up in a white gown (to remember Lucy's purity) with a red sash (to mark her martyrdom) and a crown of candles (like she is said to have worn through the catacombs). Today, this little Saint Lucy feeds her family coffee and lussekatter, tasty saffron and cardamom buns.

Lussekatter, which translates to "Lucy's cats" are also known in Sweden as lussebullar. In Denmark they go by the name luciabrød and in Finland, luciapullat. A variety of folk traditions exist to explain where the reference to Lucy's cats came from. Some say the shape looks like a curled-up cat or the twists of a cat's tail, or that the raisins look like a cat's eyes.

Prior to the Gregorian calendar, Nordic countries celebrated the winter solstice on December 13, so it's likely the Saint Lucy's traditions merged with older folk traditions. Some claim the bun was originally called dövelskatter, which translates to "devil's cat," associated with a pagan winter feast in the Netherlands. Saint Lucy's feast day, then, is a day to focus on the light that overcomes the darkness—both Lucy's candles in the darkness of the catacombs and the light of Christ coming into the world.[2]

DOUGH

1	cup (8 ounces) milk
6	cardamom pods, crushed
	Pinch saffron
5	cups (1 pound, 5.25 ounces) all-purpose or bread flour
1/4	cup (1.8 ounces) granulated sugar
1	tablespoon instant yeast
2	teaspoons kosher salt
2	eggs
8	tablespoons (4 ounces) unsalted butter, softened and cut into 1/4-inch cubes
40	golden raisins

TOPPING

Egg wash

---

1. Pour the milk into a small saucepot and add the cardamom pods and saffron. Heat the milk over medium heat until it scalds (just begins to bubble and rise inside the pot), then turn off the heat and let cool until just slightly warm to the touch (about 100°F).

2. Mix the flour, sugar, yeast, and salt in a medium-sized mixing bowl. Create a well in the center of the flour.

3. Strain the spices out of the milk, and pour the milk into the well in the flour mixture, along with the eggs and butter.

4. Mix the ingredients with your hand until the flour is hydrated. You might have to squeeze the dough to help distribute the butter all the way through. Knead the dough inside the bowl using a method similar to the stretch-and-fold technique described in part 2. Once the dough has come together, you can turn it onto the counter to knead until the dough is smooth and passes the windowpane test.

5. Once the dough is smooth, place it back in the bowl. Cover and let it rest at room temperature until doubled in size—about 1–1 1/2 hours.

6. Once the dough has risen, divide it into 20 pieces that are about 2 ounces each. Roll each piece of dough into a 10-inch snake, tapering the width of the snake near each end. Place a golden raisin at each end of the snake, one on the right and one on the left, then roll the dough around the raisins until it forms an *S* shape.

7. Place the buns on two baking sheets, about 4 inches apart, cover with a damp tea towel, and let rest for a final 30-minute proof, or until you can gently poke the dough with one finger and the indentation slowly fills in about halfway. While the buns rest, preheat the oven to 325°F.

8. When the buns have finished their final proof, brush them with the egg wash and bake for 15 minutes, or until golden brown on top.

9. Let cool and enjoy dunked in a cup of coffee or just on their own.

Slavski Kolac

Feast of Saint Nicholas (December 6 in the West; December 19 in the East)

Difficulty Level: ++

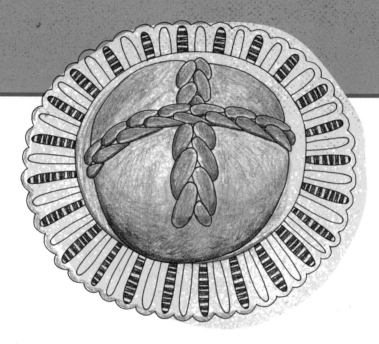

IN THE SERBIAN ORTHODOX CHURCH, each family celebrates a day called Slava on the feast day of their family's patron saint. The practice began when Christianity was introduced to Serbia, replacing a similar folk celebration. Each family chose the saint on whose feast day they were baptized, and families have continued to celebrate that saint for generations since.

On the day before the celebration, the woman of the house makes an elaborate bread mixed with consecrated water, as well as a dish of boiled wheat berries, called koljivo. The wheat is a symbol of Jesus' resurrection, harkening back to Jesus' exhortation in the gospel of John that if a grain of wheat falls to the ground and dies, it bears much fruit. It's also a reminder of the connection between the living and the departed family members who are alive in Christ.

While the bread and the wheat berries are the only dishes required at a Slava, the family typically prepares a full feast for guests as well, which is served on a table with a tall candle stamped with the image of the saint.

On the morning of the feast, the bread is brought to church, where it is blessed by the priest and sprinkled with wine. The bread is then brought home and consumed with the full feast—a reminder of the continuity between the Communion table and our tables at home. Sometimes the priest even comes to the home to bless the bread at the dinner table instead of in the church.

Many families in Serbia have Saint Nicholas, or Sveti Nikola, as their patron saint. His feast day in the Orthodox calendar is December 19 (December 6 on the Western calendar). This means almost everyone is either hosting or invited to a Slava on that day.

In the Orthodox church, a Slava that falls in a fasting season—such as Saint Nicholas Day during the Nativity Fast—must be celebrated with a feast that fits within the fasting regulations, serving food without meat, dairy, or eggs. Of course, limitation is perfect for human creativity, which means Serbians have developed all kinds of elaborate dishes to serve on this day. In accordance with these restrictions, my recipe for slavski kolac is made without animal products.

DOUGH

- 8 cups (2 pounds, 2 ounces) all-purpose or bread flour
- 1/4 cup (1.8 ounces) granulated sugar
- 2 teaspoons instant yeast
- 2 teaspoons kosher salt
- 2 cups (16 ounces) water, just warm to the touch
- 1/4 cup (2 ounces) olive oil

TOPPING

Egg wash (if you would like to keep this bread completely free from animal products, you can brush the dough with nondairy milk or oil instead)

1. In a large bowl, mix the flour, sugar, yeast, and salt.

2. Form a well in the middle of the flour mixture and add the water and olive oil.

3. Begin by thickening the water, pulling in a small amount of flour at a time. Once the water begins to thicken, about the viscosity of papier-mâché, pull in more flour and knead inside the bowl until all the flour is hydrated. Let the dough rest for 20 minutes.

4. After the dough has finished its autolyse, turn the dough onto the counter and knead for 10–12 minutes, until the dough is smooth and passes the windowpane test. If you or the dough get exhausted mid-knead, feel free to rest for 2–3 minutes before resuming.

5. Let the dough rise at room temperature, covered with plastic wrap or a damp tea towel, until doubled in size, about 1 1/2–2 hours.

6. When the dough has finished rising, turn it onto the counter. Cut off one-fourth of the dough and set aside. Shape the rest of the dough into a round and place inside an 8-inch cake pan sprayed with pan spray. Divide the reserved dough into 6 pieces and roll them into 8-inch snakes. Create 2 thin braids from the pieces. Drape the braids over the bread in the shape of a cross.

7. Cover the dough and let rise for about 45 more minutes, until you can gently poke the dough with one finger and the indentation slowly fills in about halfway. While the dough rises, preheat the oven to 325°F.

8. Once the dough is finished with its final proof, brush with egg wash and bake for 35–40 minutes, until the crust is golden brown and the loaf sounds hollow when thumped.

9. Let cool, slice, and enjoy. (Boiled wheat berries and the blessing of the priest optional.)

Concha

Las Posadas (December 16–24) | Difficulty Level: +++ | Makes 12 rolls

THE MEXICAN CELEBRATION OF LAS POSADAS begins on December 16 and carries on through December 24, a commemoration of Mary and Joseph's search for a place to stay. The practice is said to have begun as a way to teach the Christmas story. For nine days, Christmas Masses would tell the story of Mary and Joseph's wandering, then after Mass, churchgoers would hit a piñata and enjoy the fruits, nuts, and candies inside.

Today, these celebrations are held in people's homes. The partygoers are split into two groups: the innkeepers, who are allowed inside, and Mary and Joseph, who must remain outdoors. After singing a reenactment of Mary and Joseph's search for a bed, everyone is finally allowed inside and the party truly begins.

Tamales and warm fruit punch are typically served, alongside pan dulce—an assortment of sweet breads.

The history of pan dulce is just as fascinating as that of Las Posadas.[3] When the Spanish introduced wheat to the Americas, the native people were unimpressed. They preferred their breads made of corn. The story goes that one day a viceroy dipped his bread in hot chocolate, a custom that quickly caught on. When the French introduced techniques such as brioche, a dough made with lots of butter and eggs, interest in wheat breads was further piqued. After the French were conquered in 1862, Mexican bakers began adapting their techniques, incorporating native ingredients such as corn flour, piloncillo (a kind of raw sugar), chocolate, vanilla, pineapple, guava, and more. They made the sweets into all kinds of whimsical and colorful shapes, such as pigs, ears of corn, and seashells.

Concha, the seashell-shaped sweet, is simple to make. I've opted to use butter for the crunchy topping, but traditionally it's made with lard. Once you've practiced the technique, consider inviting friends over for a Las Posadas celebration of your own.

DOUGH

- 5 cups (1 pound, 5.25 ounces) all-purpose or bread flour
- 1/4 cup (1.8 ounces) granulated sugar
- 1 tablespoon instant yeast
- 2 teaspoons kosher salt
- 1 cup (8 ounces) milk
- 2 eggs
- 8 tablespoons (4 ounces) unsalted butter, softened and cut into 1/4-inch cubes

TOPPING

- 1 cup (4.25 ounces) all-purpose or bread flour
- 1 cup (4 ounces) powdered sugar
- 1 teaspoon cinnamon
- 8 tablespoons (4 ounces) unsalted butter, softened and cut into 1/4-inch cubes

1. In a large bowl, mix the 5 cups flour, granulated sugar, yeast, and salt.

2. Heat milk for 30 seconds in the microwave to remove the chill. You can also heat milk over the stove on low until just barely warm to the touch.

3. Form a well in the middle of the flour and add the milk, eggs, and 1/2 cup butter.

4. Mix the ingredients with your hand until the flour is hydrated. You might have to squeeze the dough to help distribute the butter all the way through. Knead the dough inside the bowl using a method similar to the stretch-and-fold technique described in part 2 of this book—it will be a bit sticky. Once the dough is manageable, you can turn it onto the counter to knead until the dough is smooth and passes the windowpane test.

5. Once the dough is smooth, place it back in the bowl, cover with plastic wrap or a damp tea towel, and let it rest at room temperature for 1 1/2 hours or until doubled in size.

6. Once the dough has risen, divide it into 12 pieces, about 3 ounces each. Shape into rounds and place them about 4 inches apart on two baking

sheets. Cover with plastic wrap or a damp tea towel and let them begin their 30-minute rise. Preheat the oven to 325°F.

7. While the buns rise, make the topping. In a small mixing bowl, combine flour, powdered sugar, and cinnamon. Add butter and combine until smooth. It should have the texture of wet sand. Divide the topping into 12 pieces, about 1 ounce each, and roll between your palms into a sphere. Flatten the spheres between two pieces of parchment paper, or against a counter dusted with flour, until 1/4-inch thick. Using a knife or a bench knife, gently peel the circles up from the counter and place one on top of each bun. They should drape over the buns and onto the sides. If they begin to crack, don't fret! Use your hands to gently press them into place on the buns.

8. Using the back edge of a paring knife, carve a design into the top of each bun to make it look like a seashell. (Don't worry if the designs seem subtle at this point. As the buns finish their final proof in the oven, the designs will open further to show off the decoration.)

9. When the buns have been resting about 30 minutes total and you can gently poke the dough with one finger and the indentation slowly fills in about halfway, place them in the oven and bake for 20 minutes. Let cool and enjoy with a cup of hot chocolate or warm spiced punch.

Christmastide

IN THE LITURGICAL CALENDAR, Christmas is a twelve-day celebration. Christmas begins on December 25 and carries on until January 5, the eve of Epiphany.

While Advent is a long season focused on preparation and waiting, Christmas celebrates Christ's arrival. God became human and dwelled among us, arriving not in a glorious manner but as a baby to a young mother who was wandering through Bethlehem without a bed.

Bethlehem means "house of bread," a foreshadowing of the baby who would continue to be present with us throughout generations—not in a human body but in the form of bread, broken and shared by the people who call themselves the Body of Christ. So how did Christmas become a twelve-day celebration? The answer is fascinating, if a bit disputed. According to one hypothesis, both December 25 and January 6 were chosen as dates to mark the birth of Jesus in order to replace or Christianize existing pagan festivals. The former was said to take the place of solstice celebrations in the West, and the latter, solstice celebrations in the East. Another hypothesis suggests that the date of Christmas was chosen based on the presumed date of Jesus' death. It was believed that Jesus was conceived and died on the same date, living a perfectly circular life. The presumed date of both his death and the annunciation of Mary was March 25 in the West and April 6 in the East. Therefore, Jesus' birth was established exactly nine months later: December 25 for Western Christians and January 6 for those in the East.

Others suggest that the early church celebrated both the birth and baptism of Jesus on January 6—two different but related kinds of birth—but eventually Christians wanted to split apart the two celebrations. Because December 25 was a folk celebration of the winter solstice, a time to mark the return of the sun, Christians decided to mark it as a celebration of the coming of the Son who brings light to the whole world. The days between the two became a full season of celebration.[4]

In the Eastern Church, January 6 continues to mark the baptism of Jesus, while in the Western church this date celebrates the Magi's visit, which we will talk about in the next section.

Many of the breads served during Christmastide contain dried fruits and nuts, which until recent years would have been rare treats, reserved for special celebrations such as Christmas.

BREATH PRAYER
INHALE: *A Savior has been born to you;*
EXHALE: *he is the Messiah, the Lord.*
Luke 2:11

COLLECT
Incarnate God,
you humbled yourself,
born as an infant
and laid in a manger.

A king crowned with
hay and the scent of
animals all around.

Like shepherds following the night star,
be with us as we search for you
in the humility of our daily bread.
Amen.

Stollen

Christmastide (December 25–January 5) | Difficulty Level: ++++

LEGEND HAS IT THAT STOLLEN first appeared in 1329 when the Bishop of Nauruburg (in what is now Germany) created a competition for bakers. He was so enthused by the bread that he designated a portion of each year's grain harvest specifically for the baking of stollen.

The Stollen Association, responsible for ensuring the purity of loaves emerging from Dresden's bakeries, claim that the first true record of the treat doesn't appear until 1474, written on a bill at Saint Bartholomew's hospital.[6] At the time, stollen referred to a simple loaf made of flour, yeast, and water, as it was made for the Advent fast. Over time, the bread also came to include spices, dried fruits, and sugar, making it a luxurious treat that still fit within the Advent restrictions on animal products.

Prince Ernst, the elector of Saxony, asked the church to revoke the prohibition of butter during fasting seasons specifically so he could enjoy a better stollen. While the initial response was no, Pope Innocent VIII finally caved in 1491, issuing a decree called the Butterbrief, which allowed the people of Dresden to pay a tax to the church rather than fast from dairy.

In 1730, Augustus the Strong asked local bakers to create a 1.8-ton stollen—so big it required the court architect to design a special oven for it. He then threw a party so his 24,000 guests could all get a taste. With this, the stollen festival was born. It's celebrated each year on the day before the second Sunday of Advent.

While the stollen festival takes place during Advent, the bread is decidedly a Christmas treat. The true name, Christstollen, comes from the bread's appearance—it's shaped to look like a baby in swaddling clothes.

I make between twenty and thirty loaves of stollen every year, selling them at a friend's annual holiday market, giving them as gifts to loved ones, and reserving two loaves for my family to eat for breakfast on Christmas Eve.

Whether you want to make one loaf or twenty, this bread is well worth the time and costly ingredients. Just make sure to plan ahead, as it is best when left to rest for two to four weeks before eating. This allows the fruits to release their juices and soak through the loaf.

DOUGH

1/2 cup (3.25 ounces) dried cherries, cut in half

1/2 cup (3.25 ounces) dried apricots, cut into quarters

1/4 cup (1.6 ounces) dried cranberries, cut in half

2 tablespoons (1 ounce) candied ginger, cut into 1/4-inch pieces

3/4 cup (6 ounces) orange juice

3/4 cup (6 ounces) rum

1/2 cup (2.3 ounces) whole-wheat flour, preferably sprouted wheat, if available

2 cups (8.5 ounces) all-purpose or bread flour, divided

1/2 cup (4 ounces) milk

3 eggs

2 tablespoons granulated sugar, divided

2 1/4 teaspoons instant yeast

3 tablespoons (2 ounces) almond paste

1/4 teaspoon kosher salt

1/2 teaspoon almond extract

8 tablespoons (4 ounces) unsalted butter, softened

TOPPING

8 tablespoons (4 ounces) unsalted butter, softened

2 cups (8 ounces) powdered sugar

1. In a small saucepot over medium-high heat, combine dried cherries, apricots, cranberries, candied ginger, orange juice, and rum. Bring the mixture to a boil, then cover the pot with a lid and turn off the heat. Let the fruit sit for an hour to soak up the juice and rum before beginning to mix your dough.

2. In a medium-sized mixing bowl, combine the wheat flour, 1 cup (4.25 ounces) of all-purpose or bread flour, milk, 1 egg, 1 tablespoon sugar, and yeast. Let sit at room temperature for 30 minutes. This step is called building a sponge.

3. While the sponge rests, in a small mixing bowl, combine almond paste, 1 tablespoon sugar, and salt. Rub the sugar and salt together with the almond paste to break it down into small pieces.

4. After the sponge has rested for 30 minutes, add the almond paste and sugar mixture to the sponge, along with the rest of the all-purpose or bread flour (1 cup, or 4.25 ounces), 2 eggs, almond extract, and 8 tablespoons butter, cut into 1/4-inch cubes.

5. Mix the ingredients with your hand until all the flour is hydrated. You might have to squeeze the dough to help distribute the butter all the way through. Knead the dough inside the bowl for 15–20 minutes using a method similar to the stretch-and-fold technique described in part 2 of this book. It will be very sticky, but this is okay—it should become smooth.

6. After the dough is mixed, let it rest for 5 minutes. While the dough rests, strain any remaining juices away from the dried fruit. You can reserve these juices for your next batch of stollen. Add the fruit to the dough and mix once more to incorporate fully.

7. Cover the dough and let it rest in the refrigerator for 2 hours. The chilled dough will be much easier to shape than at room temperature.

8. After the cold rest, turn the dough onto a lightly floured countertop. Gently press into an 8-inch by 12-inch rectangle, with the short side running parallel to you. Fold in the top two corners so the top edges meet and form a point. Next, fold down the point at the top two inches. Using the heel of your hand, press the folded side into the dough to seal it. Roll the top down, as if you're rolling a cinnamon roll, pressing the folded side into the dough as you go. Once you've rolled all the dough, you should have a cylindrical loaf.

9. Place the loaf on a baking sheet and cover with plastic wrap or a damp tea towel and let rest at room temperature for 30 minutes, until you can gently poke the dough with one finger and the indentation slowly fills in halfway. While the dough rests, preheat the oven to 350°F.

10. Bake the loaf for 30–40 minutes, until golden brown.

11. While the bread bakes, in a medium saucepot, melt 8 tablespoons butter over medium-low heat. After the butter melts, allow it to continue cooking.

When it begins to foam, stir gently but continuously. The milk solids will begin to turn brown and take on a nutty smell. When you can see brown specks in the bottom of the pan, turn off the heat.

12. After the bread is finished baking, let it cool for five minutes. It will split on top—this is okay. After cooling, brush the bread generously on all sides with the browned butter. Sprinkle half of the powdered sugar onto a large plate, then place the buttered stollen on top. Sprinkle the bread with the rest of the powdered sugar, then let it sit until it has cooled completely.

13. Once the bread has cooled, wrap it tightly in plastic wrap. Let it rest at room temperature for 2–4 weeks to allow the fruits to release their juices, then slice and enjoy!

Krendl

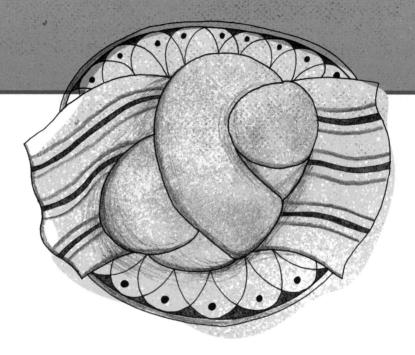

IF YOU LOOK CLOSELY, you'll notice that the Russian treat krendl is shaped a bit like a pretzel. The bread has its origins in the city of Vyborg, right on Russia's border with Finland. The story goes that Franciscan monks brought spices to the town, along with the practice of making pretzels that were boiled and then baked. The bakers of Vyborg decided to combine these new spices and this new baking technique, resulting in a spiced pretzel.

Some say the very practice of making pretzels began in the city of Vyborg. During a siege, the people began to go hungry, so monks prayed for God's help.

It rained flour, and as an expression of thanks, the monks shaped their loaves to look like hands in prayer.

Whatever the true story may be, the sweet, spiced pretzel-shaped breads made their way across the country. Over time, they evolved into a more tender loaf, stuffed with a dried fruit filling and dusted with powdered sugar. The dough is similar to the kulich dough made at Easter, though the abundance of dried fruits are in keeping with breads associated with Christmas.

DOUGH

1/4 cup (1.5 ounces) dried apricots, cut into quarters

1/4 cup (1.5 ounces) dried cherries, cut in half

1/4 cup (1.4 ounces) dried cranberries

1/4 cup (1.4 ounces) golden raisins

4 tablespoons (2 ounces) granulated sugar + 2 teaspoons granulated sugar, divided

1 cup (8 ounces) apple juice

Zest of 1 lemon

3 cups (12.75 ounces) all-purpose or bread flour

1 1/2 teaspoons instant yeast

1 teaspoon kosher salt

1/2 cup (4 ounces) milk

1 egg

4 tablespoons (2 ounces) unsalted butter, softened and cut into 1/4-inch cubes

TOPPING

1/4 cup (1 ounce) powdered sugar

1. In a small saucepot over medium-high heat, combine dried apricots, cherries, cranberries, golden raisins, 2 tablespoons sugar, apple juice, and lemon zest. Bring to a boil, then reduce to a simmer. Cook for about 20 minutes, stirring regularly, until the fruit begins to break down into a thick jam. The fruits will still be chunky, but the mixture should stick together. After cooking, turn off the heat and transfer the jam to a bowl to cool.

2. While the jam cooks, mix the dough. In a large bowl, mix the flour, 2 tablespoons plus 2 teaspoons granulated sugar, yeast, and salt.

3. Heat milk for 30 seconds in the microwave to remove the chill. You can also heat milk over the stove on low until just barely warm to the touch.

4. Form a well in the middle of the flour mixture and add the milk, egg, and butter.

5. Mix the ingredients with your hand until the flour is hydrated. You might have to squeeze the dough to help distribute the butter all the way through.

Knead the dough inside the bowl using a method similar to the stretch-and-fold technique described in part 2 of this book. It will be a bit sticky. Once the dough is manageable, you can turn it onto the counter to knead until the dough is smooth and passes the windowpane test.

6. Once the dough is smooth, place it back in the bowl, cover with plastic wrap or a damp tea towel, and let it rest at room temperature for 1 1/2 hours or until doubled in size.

7. Once the dough has risen, turn it onto a lightly floured counter and roll it out into an 8-inch by 16-inch rectangle, with the long edges running parallel to your body.

8. Spread the dried fruit filling over the dough, then roll the dough toward you. Using the heel of your hand, press the seams together to seal, then twist the dough into the shape of a pretzel. Cover with plastic wrap or a damp tea towel and let rest for 30 minutes, until you can gently poke the dough with one finger and the indentation slowly fills in halfway. While the dough rests, preheat the oven to 325°F.

9. Bake the bread for 30 minutes, until golden brown on top. Let cool, then dust with powdered sugar before slicing and serving. I enjoy mine with a cup of black tea.

Christopsomo

Christmastide (December 25–January 5) | Difficulty Level: ++

HAILING FROM GREECE, Christopsomo (pronounced "hree-STOHP-soh-moh") translates to "Christ's bread." It is made as an offering to Christ as well as a prayer for blessing and fertility. The top is decorated with an *X* (the Greek letter *chi*, which represents Christ) and a cross. The loaf usually contains a whole walnut as well, meant to represent the womb of Mary as well as the cave where Christ was born.

The exact shape and decorations vary by region. Some bakers include designs to represent the life and work of the family who will be eating it. For instance, the Sarakatsonai make an elaborate bread decorated with scenes from a shepherd's life. As nomadic cattle breeders, the Sarakatsonoi feel a particular connection to Jesus being born among animals and the revelation of his coming to the shepherds.

On the island of Crete, the women sing a song as they knead: "Christ is born, the light rises, so the yeast will come alive."[7]

Christopsomo is typically made by the woman of the house on Christmas Eve, then blessed and distributed by the man of the house on Christmas Day. The loaf is meant to serve as a reminder of the bread shared at Communion, marking the unity of Christ's church.

DOUGH

- 8 cups (2 pounds, 2 ounces) all-purpose or bread flour
- 2 teaspoons instant yeast
- 2 teaspoons kosher salt
- 1/2 teaspoon mahlab, optional
- 1/2 teaspoon star anise
- 1 3/4 cups (14 ounces) water, just warm to the touch
- 1/4 cup (2 ounces) olive oil
- 1/4 cup (3 ounces) honey
- 1/2 cup (2 ounces) lightly toasted walnuts, chopped

TOPPING

- Egg wash
- 2 tablespoons honey
- 1 teaspoon sesame seeds
- Whole walnut, in its shell (optional)

1. In a large bowl, mix the flour, yeast, salt, and spices.

2. Form a well in the middle of the flour and add the water, olive oil, and honey.

3. Begin by thickening the water, pulling in a small amount of flour at a time. Once the water begins to thicken, about the viscosity of papier-mâché, pull in more flour and knead inside the bowl until all the flour is hydrated. Let the dough rest for 20 minutes.

4. After the dough has finished its autolyse, turn the dough onto the counter and knead for 10–12 minutes, until smooth. Cut off one-fourth of the dough and place in a small bowl, covered with plastic wrap or a damp tea towel. Sprinkle the walnuts over the rest of the dough and knead until incorporated.

5. Let the dough rise at room temperature, covered with plastic wrap or a damp tea towel, until doubled in size—about 1 1/2–2 hours.

6. When the dough has finished rising, turn it onto the counter. Shape the main portion of the dough into a round and place inside an 8-inch cake pan sprayed generously with pan spray. With the reserved dough, make two thin 8-inch braids and any other designs you want to include. Drape the braids over the bread in the shape of a cross and add your additional decorations.

7. Cover the dough and let rise for about 45 minutes, until you can gently poke the dough with one finger and the indentation slowly fills in about halfway. While the dough rises, preheat the oven to 325°F. Once the dough is finished with its final proof, brush with egg wash and bake for 35–40 minutes, until the crust is golden brown and the loaf sounds hollow when thumped.

8. As soon as the bread comes out of the oven, brush it with honey and sprinkle with sesame seeds. Let the bread cool, then serve. If you'd like, you can nestle a whole walnut in its shell in the center of the cross. If desired, you can do this before the final proof and baking.

A NOTE ON MAHLAB

Mahlab is a spice common throughout the Mediterranean made from the ground pits of Mahlab cherries. It adds a flavor that is a bit floral, a bit like bitter almond, and a bit like cherry. You can purchase it online from a variety of spice purveyors, but my favorite is Curio Spice Co. Their mahlab comes whole and you can grind it yourself in a spice grinder or with a mortar and pestle. If you can't find mahlab, feel free to leave it out of this recipe.

Moravian Sugar Cake

Christmastide (December 25–January 5) | Difficulty Level: +++

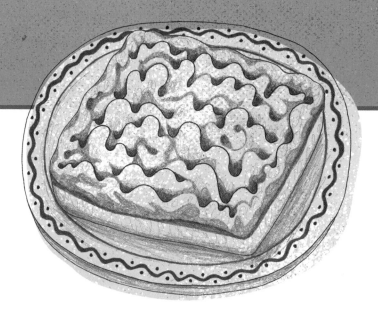

MORAVIANS ARE PROUD TO SAY that they were the first Protestants. They trace their roots back to the teachings of John Hus, who led a reformation in Moravia (modern-day Czech Republic), in the early fifteenth century. Three hundred years later, a group of Moravians moved to the United States, settling first in Pennsylvania, where Bethlehem became their northern headquarters, and later adding a southern headquarters in Salem (now Winston-Salem), North Carolina, where many of their historic homes and shops are still in active use.[8]

Perhaps the most well-known of Moravian traditions is the Love Feast, a practice that caught the attention of John Wesley, who brought the tradition into Methodism. A Moravian Love Feast is reminiscent of the bread and wine shared in Communion, signaling the ways the community built through the Lord's Table flows into our daily tables as well. A Moravian Love Feast is a service of song and prayer alongside a meal of coffee and bread, typically a sweet bread of some kind.

In North Carolina, where I live, Moravians are commonly associated with their sugar cake. Originally served as an Easter treat, this dimpled bread filled with pockets of butter and sugar soon became the bread of choice for any special occasion, especially the Love Feast. Today, it is most often served at Christmas, whether bought at the historic bakery in Old Salem, at a local Moravian church fundraiser, or made from scratch at home. Legend has it that Moravian men used to seek out wives with thick fingers, which would create wider divots in the dough to hold more sugar cake topping.

Moravian Sugar Cake is made using mashed potatoes. Potato starch holds more water than the starches in wheat, increasing the moisture content in the dough. This keeps the bread tender, even days after baking. Some bakers simplify the process using instant mashed potatoes, but I'm convinced the best sugar cakes are made the old-fashioned way.

DOUGH

1   russet potato, peeled, boiled, and mashed (1/2 cup mashed potato)

1/4   cup (2 ounces) water, ideally reserved from boiling the potato

4   cups (1 pound, 1 ounce) all-purpose or bread flour

1/4   cup (1.8 ounces) granulated sugar

11/2   teaspoons instant yeast

1   teaspoon kosher salt

1/2   cup (4 ounces) milk

6   tablespoons (3 ounces) unsalted butter, softened and cut into 1/4-inch cubes

1   egg

TOPPING

8   tablespoons (4 ounces) unsalted butter, melted

1/2   cup (3.6 ounces) granulated sugar

1/2   cup (3.6 ounces) light brown sugar

1   teaspoon cinnamon

1/4   teaspoon kosher salt

1. After peeling, boiling, and mashing the potato, measure 1/2 cup of mashed potato for use in this recipe. Reserve 1/4 cup of the boiling water for use in the recipe as well. While using the boiling water is optional, this increases the tenderness of the dough even more.

2. In a large bowl, mix the flour, 1/4 cup sugar, yeast, and salt. Form a well in the center of the flour and add the potato, milk, and water. Next, add the 6 tablespoons of cubed butter and the egg.

3. Mix the ingredients with your hand until the flour is hydrated. You might have to squeeze the dough to help distribute the butter all the way through. Knead the dough inside the bowl using a method similar to the stretch-and-fold technique described in part 2 of this book. It will be a bit sticky. Once the dough is manageable, you can turn it onto the counter to knead until the dough is smooth and passes the windowpane test.

4. Once the dough is smooth, place it back in the bowl, cover with plastic wrap or a damp tea towel, and let it rest at room temperature for 1 1/2 hours or until doubled in size.

5. After the dough has doubled in size, turn it onto a sprayed or lined baking tray with 1-inch sides. If you don't have a baking tray, you can also use a 9×13-inch pan. This will result in a thicker cake and may increase the bake time slightly. Press the dough out to the edges of the pan. If it begins to spring back instead of spreading, let it rest for a few minutes to allow the gluten to relax before trying again. Cover the pan and let the dough rest another half hour. While the dough rests, preheat the oven to 325°F.

6. After the dough has finished this second rise, press your fingers into the top of the dough to create dimples all across the surface. Pour the 8 tablespoons of melted butter over the dough, allowing it to settle into the wells formed by your fingers. In a small bowl, mix the 1/2 cup granulated sugar, brown sugar, cinnamon, and salt, then sprinkle on top of the butter.

7. Bake the bread for 25 minutes, let cool, and enjoy—preferably with a mug of coffee and in the company of your church congregation in a service of hymns.

Epiphany

ONE YEAR DURING THE COFFEE HOUR AT MY CHURCH, the staff brought in several king cakes on January 6. After every crumb had been consumed (the children were especially thrilled with the sugar rush), a congregant said to me, "I'm confused. I'm so glad we had king cake today, but I thought it was a Mardi Gras thing."

Mardi Gras, also known as Shrove Tuesday or Fat Tuesday, is the day before the start of Lent. It's a day, or sometimes a few days, of parades and rich foods, of masks and beads and debauchery. But the Fat Tuesday celebration is actually the culmination of a season that starts on January 6, spanning from Epiphany all the way to Lent. In many places around the world, this season is called Carnival. It's also known as Epiphanytide or Ordinary I—the first season of Ordinary time.

In the Western church, the feast of Epiphany marks the manifestation of Christ to the Gentiles, when kings bowed before a baby whose bed was a manger. An infant born in poverty, whom they recognized as their true king. When King Herod learned that the magi were going to worship the baby, he felt threatened. The Lord warned Mary and Joseph of King Herod's planned massacre and directed them to flee to Egypt.

This story is one of social upheaval, a subversion of the expected order. It's a story of kings bowing to a child. Of a powerful earthly king who was afraid of being dethroned by a poor infant. When we celebrate Epiphany, we remember that God's ways are often unexpected. They are delightfully ironic, turning our sense of order on its head.

Epiphany is also a season of hospitality. We remember the hospitality of the kings who bowed to Jesus and gave him gifts. We consider the hospitality the Holy Family might have received in Egypt. And most of all, we recognize the hospitality of God by welcoming Gentiles into the family of God. We then commit our own homes as places of hospitality for the coming year by writing 20 + C + M + B + [the year] in chalk above the doorframe.

The C + M + B stands for the Latin phrase *Christus mansionem benedicat*, which means "May Christ bless this house." The letters can also represent the traditional names given to the Magi: Caspar, Melchior, and Balthazar. It's a way of asking God to make our homes a place of rest and safety for all who come through our doors.

The season of Carnival, which runs from Epiphany to the start of Lent, was not likely practiced by early Christians. Most evidence suggests that these celebrations began in Europe around the thirteenth century, with the different regional traditions shaped by the late-winter folk festivals of each place. To this day, it's celebrated all over the world in areas with a strong Christian presence, most notably Europe and South, Central, and Caribbean America. Some of the most famous celebrations take place in Rio de Janeiro and Venice.

Carnival especially took off in places where Christianity was spread under colonial rule, because it was a way for those who were colonized to reclaim agency and mock those who had asserted control over them—without the rulers understanding what was really taking place.

Masks and shared foods provide the illusion of egalitarianism between the poor and the elite, while in fact they create an opportunity for the poor to reveal the absurdity of the ones who claim power over them (kind of like the emperor without his clothes).

Carnival is a time of preparation for the celebration to come at Easter. These festivities reveal the need for Christ's death, which unseats the power of sin and death and allows for a fuller celebration of his resurrection and our freedom. They remind us what we're waiting for while we fast, and they also remind us that true celebration is impossible without repentance.

The foods of this season are directly tied to Lent and the traditional food restrictions during that season. Not only do the rich foods fit with Carnival's reputation for excessive consumption, they serve as a means of preventing waste. All the foods popular in the pre-Lenten celebrations were ways to use up the stores of butter, milk, and eggs people had on hand so they wouldn't go to waste during the fast.

BREATH PRAYER

INHALE: *We saw his star when it rose*

EXHALE: *and have come to worship him.*

> *Matthew 2:2*

COLLECT

God of surprises,
you delight in
flipping expectations
on their head—
a king threatened by
an infant who unseats
the power of sin and death.

As we open our doors and
share this bread, may we see you
in surprising ways too.
Amen.

King Cake

Epiphany (January 6–Shrove Tuesday) | Difficulty Level: ++++

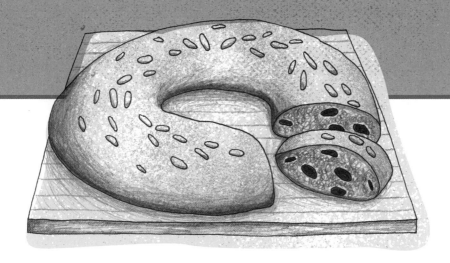

I ATE MY FIRST KING CAKE in elementary school. A classmate whose family was from Louisiana brought it in to share. She told us about the baby figurine hidden inside—representing baby Jesus, hiding from King Herod—which one lucky person would find in their slice. We all devoured our pieces, hoping we'd get to be the king or queen for a day. But once a classmate found the trinket, he panicked. The tradition goes that whoever finds the baby has to provide the cake the following year, and he didn't know where he could buy one.

There are many versions of king cake, including the French galette des rois (a puff pastry cake with frangipane filling), the Spanish rosca de reyes, or the Portuguese bolo rei (both brioche-style breads studded with candied fruits). Louisiana style is a brioche cake filled with cream cheese and covered in purple, gold, and green sprinkles meant to signify justice, power, and faith.

Each style of king cake holds one thing in common: a hidden trinket, such as a bean, coin, or plastic baby. In some traditions, the person who finds the trinket provides the king cake the following year, though in Mexico, whoever finds the trinket in their rosca de reyes must provide the tamales on Candlemas (a holiday we will talk about in the next recipe).

Some bakers in the southern United States have begun developing what they call queen cakes, merging techniques from the traditional forms and incorporating flavors local to their own home. The recipe I've developed follows this queen cake tradition of merging techniques and preferred flavors. I use a brioche-style dough and fill it with an almond frangipane filling and dried cherries. Then I stud the top with nuts and top with powdered sugar.

DOUGH

2 1/2	cups (10.6 ounces) all-purpose or bread flour
2	tablespoons + 2 teaspoons granulated sugar
1 1/2	teaspoons instant yeast
1	teaspoon kosher salt
1/2	cup (4 ounces) milk
2	eggs
8	tablespoons (4 ounces) unsalted butter, softened and cut into 1/4-inch cubes

FRANGIPANE

4	tablespoons (2 ounces) unsalted butter, softened
1/4	cup (1.8 ounces) granulated sugar
1/2	cup (2 ounces) almond flour or almond meal
1	egg
2	teaspoons almond extract
1	tablespoon + 1 teaspoon all-purpose flour
1/4	teaspoon kosher salt

ADDITIONAL FILLING

1/2	cup (1.7 ounces) dried cherries, cut in half
	Large dried bean, whole unshelled nut, or baby figurine

TOPPING

	Egg wash
1/4	cup (1 ounce) sliced almonds
1/4	cup (1 ounce) powdered sugar

---

1. In a large bowl, mix the flour, sugar, yeast, and salt.

2. Heat milk for 30 seconds in the microwave to remove the chill. You can also heat milk on low over the stove until just barely warm to the touch.

3. Form a well in the middle of the flour mixture and add the milk and the 2 eggs. Mix the ingredients with your hand until the flour is hydrated, then knead the dough inside the bowl using a method similar to the stretch-and-fold technique described in part 2 of this book.

4. Once the gluten has begun to form, mix in 8 tablespoons of butter. Squeeze the dough to help distribute the butter all the way through. It will be very sticky. Let the dough rest for 30 minutes.

5. After the dough has had a 30-minute rest, stretch and fold the dough 16–20 times, then cover with plastic wrap or a damp tea towel and let chill in the refrigerator for 4–12 hours.

6. Just before you are ready to shape the dough, mix the frangipane. In a medium-sized mixing bowl, combine 4 tablespoons of butter and 1/4 cup of sugar and mix until smooth. Add the almond flour, egg, almond extract, flour, and salt, and mix again until smooth.

7. Turn your dough onto a lightly floured countertop. Flour the top of the dough as well, then roll with a rolling pin to a 10-inch by 18-inch rectangle, with the long edges running parallel to your body. Spread the frangipane over the dough, leaving an inch-wide border on both long sides. Sprinkle the dried cherries on top. Place the bean, nut, or baby figurine somewhere on the dough, then gently roll the dough, pinching the seam together with your fingers to seal the filling inside. Pull the ends together to create a circle, and pinch the ends together.

8. Cover with plastic wrap or a damp tea towel and let rest at room temperature for 45 minutes to an hour, until you can gently poke the dough with one finger and the indentation slowly fills in halfway. While the dough rests, preheat the oven to 325°F.

9. When the dough is ready for the oven, brush with egg wash and sprinkle with sliced almonds. Bake for 30 minutes, until golden brown. Let cool, then dust with powdered sugar. Slice and serve.

Saint Brigid's Oat Bread

Feast of Saint Brigid (February 1–2) | Difficulty Level: +

THE BEGINNING OF FEBRUARY falls halfway between the winter solstice and spring equinox. As we discussed at the beginning of this section, pre-
industrial agrarian societies kept a close eye on the movements of the sun and
moon to situate themselves in time. As a result, folk traditions connected to the
start of February exist all around the world.

In Christian tradition, February 2 is Candlemas—a celebration of the presen-
tation of Jesus at the Temple, which would have taken place forty days after his
birth, as well as a celebration of the purification of Mary. In Mexico, Candlemas
is celebrated with tamales (provided by the lucky one who found the trinket in
their rosca de reyes on January 6), carried over from the pre-Christian folk holiday celebrated on this day.

In Ireland, Candlemas also marks the celebration of the Feast Day of Saint Brigid of Kildare, a fifth-century woman known for her incredible generosity. Saint Brigid was named after the Celtic goddess of fertility, who has long been celebrated on February 2—called Imbolc in pagan tradition. Irish Christians took this as an opportunity to celebrate a woman of the same name.

Saint Brigid was born into slavery to a Christian mother and a Druid father, but her generosity tired her master—Brigid fed anyone she met who had need. She was put in charge of the dairy, and somehow, despite giving so much food away, the dairy prospered.

Saint Brigid took a vow of chastity (though Saint Patrick is said to have accidentally gotten his papers mixed up, using the vow for ordination instead!) and founded a monastery in Kildare built above a pagan shrine to the goddess of the same name.

Bannock, or oat bread, has long been eaten on this day. In folk tradition, a loaf was left out for the goddess Brigid to ask for blessings of fertility, prosperity, and health. The bread was cut into quarters to mark the fact that February 2 is a quarter day, falling between a solstice and an equinox. Irish Christians instead focus on the marking as a sign of the cross, asking for God's protection and blessing.

The oat bread is typically served with honey and butter (preferably churned on the same day!), a reminder of both Brigid's miraculous way with cows and the Promised Land, which the book of Exodus describes as a land flowing with milk and honey.

DOUGH

3/4 cup (2.5 ounces) rolled oats

1/2 cup (4 ounces) buttermilk

3/4 cup (3.2 ounces) all-purpose flour

1/4 cup (1.1 ounce) whole-wheat flour

1 tablespoon granulated sugar

3/4 teaspoon baking powder

1/4 teaspoon baking soda

1/2 teaspoon kosher salt

8 tablespoons (4 ounces) unsalted butter, frozen and grated

1 egg

1. In a small bowl, soak oats in buttermilk for 20–30 minutes.

2. While the oats soak, preheat the oven to 350°F. In a medium-sized mixing bowl, combine flours, sugar, baking powder, baking soda, and salt.

3. Add the butter to the bowl and rub together with the flour, working quickly to avoid warming the butter. The mixture should be mealy, not smooth.

4. Add the oat mixture and the egg to the flour mixture and stir until combined.

5. Pour the mixture onto a baking sheet lined with parchment paper or a silicone mat, or pour it onto a cast-iron skillet. Moisten your fingers and smooth the dough into a circle about 8 inches in diameter. Cut a 1/4-inch-deep score in the shape of a cross across the top of the dough.

6. Bake for 30 minutes. Let cool and serve, smeared with butter, drizzled with honey, and sprinkled with salt. This recipe is a great excuse to splurge on golden Irish butter!

Semlor

Shrove Tuesday (the Tuesday before the start of Lent) | Difficulty Level: ++++

Makes 14 buns

SEMLOR (OR THE SINGULAR, SEMLA) ARE SWEDISH TREATS served on Fat Tuesday. They are sweet rolls whose insides are scooped out and mixed with milk and almond paste to form a custard. After the mixture gets spooned back into the roll, the dessert gets a hefty dollop of whipped cream and a sprinkling of powdered sugar.

Sometimes semlor are served in a bowl, floating in hot milk. I've never tried them this way, but I think I prefer to consume mine alongside a mug of steaming coffee, avoiding a soggy-bottomed roll.

Semlor are believed to have started out as a way for people to use stale bread, soaking the loaf in milk to soften it up again. Over time, the bread was stuffed with additional treats such as raisins and other dried fruits. Around the sixteenth century, the practice of scooping out the insides of the roll and mixing them with cream, almonds, and sugar emerged.

Swedish lore recounts the fateful day in 1771 when King Adolf Frederick ate fourteen semlor soaked in milk, alongside lobster, caviar, and champagne. That same day he died . . . of indigestion.

In response, the poet Johan Gabriel Oxenstierna wrote that Fat Tuesday should be prohibited and the Lenten bun expelled from Sweden, as it had committed regicide.

I would argue that this story epitomizes what the season of Carnival is meant to do: expose the grotesqueness of worldly excess so we can properly celebrate the risen King.

DOUGH

2 1/2	cups (10.6 ounces) all-purpose or bread flour
2	tablespoons + 2 teaspoons granulated sugar
1 1/2	teaspoons instant yeast
1	teaspoon kosher salt
1/2	cup (4 ounces) milk
2	eggs
8	tablespoons (4 ounces) unsalted butter, softened and cut into 1/4-inch cubes

TOPPING 1

Egg wash

FILLING 1

8 1/2	tablespoons (6 ounces) almond paste
3	tablespoons (1.5 ounces) milk

FILLING 2

1	cup (8 ounces) heavy cream
1/2	teaspoon granulated sugar

TOPPING 2

1	tablespoon powdered sugar

---

1. In a large bowl, mix the flour, sugar, yeast, and salt.

2. Heat milk for 30 seconds in the microwave to remove the chill. You can also heat milk over the stove on low until just barely warm to the touch.

3. Form a well in the middle of the flour mixture and add the milk and eggs. Mix the ingredients with your hand until the flour is hydrated, then knead

the dough inside the bowl using a method similar to the stretch-and-fold technique described in part 2 of this book.

4. Once the gluten has begun to form, mix in the butter. Squeeze the dough to help distribute the butter all the way through. It will be very sticky. Let the dough rest for 30 minutes at room temperature.

5. After the dough has had a 30-minute rest, stretch and fold the dough 16–20 times, then cover with plastic wrap or a damp tea towel and let chill in the refrigerator for 4–12 hours.

6. Once the dough is finished with its cold rest, divide the dough into 14 pieces, about 1 1/2 ounces each. Shape each piece into a round. Place the buns on two baking sheets lined with parchment paper or a silicone mat. Cover with plastic wrap or a damp tea towel and let rest at room temperature for 45 minutes to an hour, until you can gently poke the dough with one finger and the indentation slowly fills in halfway. While the dough rests, preheat the oven to 325°F.

7. Just before putting the buns in the oven, brush them with egg wash. Bake for 15–20 minutes, until golden brown. Let cool.

8. When the buns have cooled, slice the top off each one. Scoop out the bread inside each bun and place in a medium-sized mixing bowl. Add the almond paste and milk, and mix until smooth. If needed, squeeze the mixture together with your hands. It will be a thick paste. Scoop the mixture back into the hollowed center of the buns.

9. In a large mixing bowl, whisk together the heavy cream and granulated sugar until stiff peaks form. Transfer the whipped cream to a piping bag and pipe cream onto each bun. If you prefer, you can simply scoop the cream with a spoon, though the piped cream looks much nicer!

10. Place the top on each bun, then dust with powdered sugar and serve— preferably not all fourteen at once.

Lent

THE SEASON OF LENT WAS OBSERVED among all Christians from the Council of Nicaea in the year 325 all the way until the Reformation. The writings of second-century church historians Irenaeus and Tertullian suggest that some kind of pre-Easter fast was the norm even before the fourth century, but Nicaea marks the start of the forty-day fast followed by most Christians to this day.

In the early church, the purpose of this fast was to serve as a long period of instruction and preparation for those who would be baptized on Easter Sunday. The fast mirrored the many forty-day fasts in Scripture, most notable among them Jesus' fast in the wilderness at the start of his ministry.

The specifics of the Lenten fast have varied over the years, with some Christians living off only bread and water, and some limiting their food intake to a single meal each day. For medieval Catholics, it was common to fast from meat and dairy, inspiring a diet of salted herring and—for those who could afford it—crystalized ginger chews to help take away the salty taste. Eastern Orthodox Christians follow a similar fasting regimen to this day, foregoing meat, dairy, and even vertebrate fish, though shellfish are allowed.

After the Reformation, some Protestants gave up the Lenten fast, since it isn't mentioned in Scripture. They worried it would lead people to think they needed to earn God's favor when, in fact, God's grace is a gift.

The season of Lent was certainly abused by some medieval clergy, who demanded that their parishioners live ascetically while they feasted in their own homes. With their focus on rooting out hypocrisy from the church, the Reformers were rightfully wary about this extrabiblical season. But in dropping the rhythm, they passed up its many gifts as well.

"Fasting is an art," writes Orthodox priest Father Milan Savich.[9] He points to God's restriction of the fruit of the tree in Eden as evidence that fasting is not a way to atone for one's sin but rather a means of recognizing the human limitations that have existed since the beginning of creation.

Fasting is not an act of penance but a way to guide us into repentance. It's about forming us as individuals and as a community to recognize our utter dependence on God and to value the good gifts of God. As we hunger for the item we've temporarily set aside, we're reminded that everything we have is a gift, a taste of the goodness of God. We can then repent of the ways we have failed to treasure God's creation as a gift, and we can draw near to God through this time of fasting as well as in our future feast.

This season of communal fasting also reminds us of our communal identity. Lent is not primarily about our individual spiritual health, although it can be individually meaningful. More importantly, it's about our participation in a community of Christians that stretches across time and around the world, as the recipes in this book are meant to reveal. It's a way to remember with our whole bodies that we are part of a community that reaches way beyond ourselves.

BREATH PRAYER

INHALE: *From dust we come,*
EXHALE: *and to dust we will return.*
Genesis 3:19

COLLECT

God who wandered in the desert,
you say that we do not live
by bread alone, but by every word
that proceeds from your mouth.

Bread of life, we follow you into
the desert this Lent, emptying ourselves
so we might be filled with your love.

Draw near to us in our fasting,
that we might fully celebrate
the coming Easter feast.
Amen.

Lagana

Clean Monday (the first day of Orthodox Lent) | Difficulty Level: +

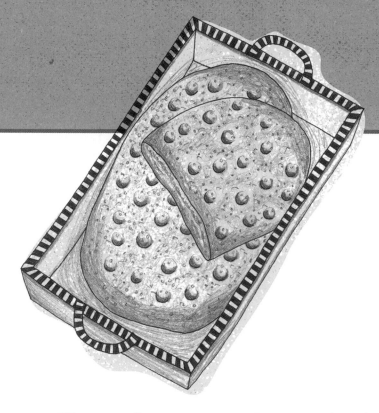

WHILE THE WESTERN CHURCH BEGINS LENT on Ash Wednesday, in the Orthodox Church, Lent begins on a Monday—Clean Monday, as it's called.

In Greece, Clean Monday is a public holiday and a day of celebration. The season of fasting is welcomed with anticipation and joy, usually with picnics and kite flying. The limitations of Lenten fasting have made way for an elaborate Clean Monday spread: olives, octopus, shrimp, mussels, halva (a crumbly sesame candy), and taramasalata (a spread made of fish roe, lemons, and olive oil).

These Clean Monday celebrations are reminders that fasting does not need to be a somber affair—after all, it's an opportunity to draw nearer to God. Instead, these limitations—meant as a reminder of our humanity—can be the fertile soil for creativity. These celebrations are also a way to remember Christ's words in Matthew 6:16: "When you fast, do not look somber as the hypocrites do" (NIV).

The most important item on a Clean Monday table is a sesame flatbread called lagana.

Lagana is a finger bread similar to focaccia or to Moravian sugar cake (the recipe can be found in the Christmastide section of this book). Historically, lagana was prepared without any leaven or oil—a nod to the unleavened bread of Passover—but over time, it became common to use both. Some bakers add herbs or olives to their lagana too.

Sometimes extra lagana dough is used to make a Mrs. Lent doll, a figure that helps keep time during the fasting season. A Mrs. Lent doll is made with a cross on her head and with hands folded in prayer. She has no mouth (to symbolize fasting) and seven legs, one for each week of Lent. Every week, the family cuts off a leg as a countdown to Easter.

DOUGH

2 1/2 cups (10.6 ounces) all-purpose or bread flour	3/4 cup (6 ounces) water, just warm to the touch
2 teaspoons instant yeast	1 tablespoon olive oil + 2 tablespoons for the baking tray
1 teaspoon granulated sugar	
1 teaspoon kosher salt	3 tablespoons sesame seeds

---

1. In a medium-sized mixing bowl, combine flour, yeast, sugar, and salt.

2. Form a well in the center of the flour mixture and add the water and 1 tablespoon olive oil. Mix the wet and dry ingredients, then knead in the bowl or on the counter for 10–12 minutes. When the dough is smooth and passes the windowpane test, place it back in the bowl, cover, and let it rise at room temperature until doubled in size, about 45 minutes.

3. When the dough has doubled in size, turn it onto a baking tray drizzled with olive oil. Flip the dough over so it has olive oil on both sides. Wet your fingers and gently press into the surface of the dough to spread it into a dimpled oval, about 12 inches long and 8 inches wide.

4. Sprinkle sesame seeds over the surface of the dough, then let it rise for 20–25 minutes more, until you can gently poke the dough with one finger and the indentation slowly fills in halfway. While the dough rests, preheat the oven to 325°F.

5. Bake for 15–20 minutes. The dough will be just slightly browned, but the crust should remain soft. Let cool and enjoy with a delicious spread of olives and shellfish!

Pretzels

Lent (the six weeks leading up to Easter) | Difficulty Level: +++
Makes 6 pretzels

WHILE THE EXACT LOCATION OF THE PRETZEL'S INVENTION is disputed (Italy? France? Germany? Russia?), most stories about the pretzel's provenance agree it was developed by a monk around the seventh century. The pretzel was designed specifically for Lent, a fun treat made without animal products to honor the Lenten restrictions.

The shape has dual meaning. The three holes represent the three persons of the Trinity: Father, Son, and Holy Spirit. The twists are also meant to look like arms in prayer—not palm pressed to palm, but hands crossed over the chest to touch the opposite shoulder. While this posture is less common today, some churches still encourage this motion when receiving a blessing. The name pretzel actually comes from the Latin term *bracellae*, which means "little arms."

Every aspect of a pretzel is a reminder that even in our fasting, our baking and eating guide us into prayer.

The tangy chew of the pretzel's crust comes from boiling the dough before baking. A true pretzel is boiled in water mixed with lye, which gelatinizes the starches on the surface of the dough and increases the Maillard reaction (the caramelization of proteins that creates an umami flavor). Since lye is difficult to come by and dangerous if used incorrectly, I boil mine in water and baking soda instead, which creates a similar reaction on the surface of the dough.

DOUGH

- 3 cups (12.75 ounces) all-purpose or bread flour
- 1 cup (4.6 ounces) whole-wheat flour
- 1 tablespoon granulated sugar
- 2 teaspoons instant yeast
- 2 teaspoons kosher salt
- 1 cup (8 ounces) water, just warm to the touch
- 2 tablespoons vegetable oil

BOILING LIQUID

- 10 cups (80 ounces) water
- 2/3 cup (2.1 ounces) baking soda

TOPPING

Egg wash

Coarse pretzel salt or flaky salt, such as Maldon or Falksalt

1. In a medium-sized mixing bowl, combine flours, sugar, yeast, and salt.

2. Create a well in the center of the flour mixture and add water and oil. Mix the wet and dry ingredients, then knead in the bowl or on the counter for 10–12 minutes. When the dough is smooth and passes the windowpane test, place it back in the bowl, cover, and let it rise at room temperature until doubled in size, about 45 minutes.

3. When the dough has risen, turn onto the counter and divide into 6 pieces, about 4 ounces each. Roll each piece of dough into a 20-inch snake. As the gluten gets tired, it will spring back, so you'll need to roll the dough in stages. Begin by rolling each piece partway, until it gets tired, then rest the dough a few minutes before repeating.

4. After each piece of dough is rolled to 20 inches, tuck the right end under the dough one-third from the left end. Next, tuck the left end under the corner formed on the right. Arrange the pretzels on a baking sheet, cover, and let rest for 30 minutes, until you can gently poke the dough with one finger and the indentation slowly fills in halfway.

5. While the dough rests, bring 10 cups of water to a boil in a large pot and preheat the oven to 375°F.

6. When the dough is ready and the water is boiling, add the baking soda to the water, then boil each pretzel for 1 minute, flipping the pretzel halfway through. Depending on the diameter of your pot, you should be able to boil 2–3 pretzels at a time. When the pretzel is done boiling, pull it out of the water with a slotted spoon and let any excess water drip off before returning the pretzel to the baking tray.

7. After all the pretzels have been boiled, brush them lightly with egg wash and sprinkle with salt.

8. Bake the pretzels for 12–15 minutes, until deep brown. Let cool and enjoy. I love mine served with mustard, sauerkraut, and (although not in keeping with historic fasting practices) a nice sausage.

Mucenici

Feast of the Forty Martyrs (March 9) | Difficulty Level: ++++

Makes 20 buns

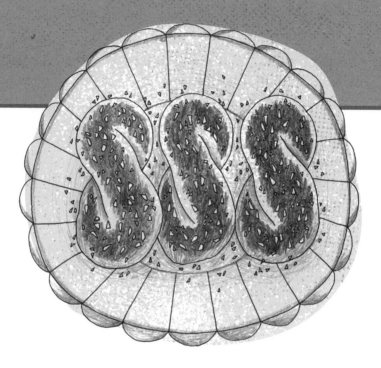

ON MARCH 9, ORTHODOX CHRISTIANS COMMEMORATE the Holy Martyrs of Sebaste. The forty martyrs were Roman soldiers who lived during the reign of Emperor Licinius in the early fourth century. They were tortured and imprisoned in Sebaste, Cappadocia (in modern-day Turkey), because they refused to recant their faith. It is said that while they were in prison, Christ visited them and encouraged them to remain strong in their faith. When they continued to refuse apostasy, they were left to die standing on a frozen lake.

The feast day was established long before the forty days of Lent, but because of its timing, it fortuitously falls during this season of fasting. The forty martyrs serve as a parallel to the forty days of Lent, encouraging believers to cling to Christ through the difficulties of fasting as we look ahead to the Resurrection.

In Romania, the Feast of the Holy Martyrs of Sebaste also marks the beginning of the agricultural year, a day when families clean their homes, burn their trash, and prepare for the season to come. They smash the ground with mallets to drive away the cold and unlock the warmth.

It is traditional to bake forty pastries on this day to commemorate the forty martyrs, though there are a few different forms of the pastry that have become associated with this day. Some bakers make a dough into the shape of skylarks, birds that sing to welcome the spring. Skylarks are also said to serve as a reminder of the Holy Spirit, who spoke to and encouraged each soldier.

In Romania, where the celebration of this feast day is particularly strong, there are two different kinds of pastries, both called mucenici (pronounced "moo-cha-NEECH"), which means "martyr." The first is similar to pasta, which gets boiled and served in sugar water and sprinkled with cinnamon. This dessert soup is said to be a reminder of the lake where the martyrs died. The second is a fluffy roll that's soaked in syrup, brushed with honey, and sprinkled with crushed walnuts.

Both versions of mucenici are shaped into a figure eight, designed to look like a person and to remind us of the eight days the martyrs were imprisoned before their death.

In the Orthodox church, the fasting restrictions of Lent are eased on the Feast of the Holy Martyrs, though the skylark and pasta versions of March 9 pastries are typically still made without animal products. The fluffy roll variety, though, is made with milk, butter, and eggs—a delicious reprieve in the midst of fasting. My recipe is the latter version, though it makes only twenty buns. If you're feeling especially ambitious (and hungry!), you can double the recipe to get the full forty pastries for the day. As you eat, take a moment to reflect on the faithful followers who have gone before us.

DOUGH

 5 cups (1 pound, 5.25 ounces) all-purpose or bread flour

1/4 cup (1.8 ounces) granulated sugar

 1 tablespoon instant yeast

 2 teaspoons kosher salt

 1 cup (8 ounces) milk

 2 eggs

 8 tablespoons (4 ounces) unsalted butter, softened and cut into 1/4-inch cubes

 1 teaspoon vanilla

 Zest of 1 lemon

TOPPING 1

 Egg wash

SYRUP

1/2 cup (3.6 ounces) granulated sugar

1/2 cup (4 ounces) water

 1 tablespoon rum

TOPPING 2

1/4 cup (3 ounces) honey

 1 cup (4.4 ounces) walnuts, pulsed to a powder

1. In a medium-sized mixing bowl, mix the flour, sugar, yeast, and salt.

2. Heat milk for 30 seconds in the microwave to remove the chill. You can also heat milk over the stove on low heat until just barely warm to the touch. Create a well in the center of the flour mixture. Pour the milk into the well, along with the eggs, butter, vanilla, and lemon zest.

3. Mix the ingredients with your hand until the flour is hydrated. You might have to squeeze the dough to help distribute the butter all the way through. Knead the dough inside the bowl using a method similar to the stretch-and-fold technique described in part 2 of this book. It will be a bit sticky. Once the dough is manageable, you can turn it onto the counter to knead until the dough is smooth and passes the windowpane test.

4. Once the dough is smooth, place it back in the bowl, cover with plastic wrap or a damp tea towel, and let it rest at room temperature for 1 1/2 hours or until doubled in size.

5. Once the dough has risen, divide it into 20 pieces that are about 2 ounces each. Roll each piece of dough into a 12-inch snake, tapering the width of the snake near the ends. Form each snake into a circle, pinching the ends together. Next, twist the circle in the center to create the shape of a figure eight.

6. Place the buns on two baking sheets, about 2 inches apart. Cover with plastic wrap or a damp tea towel and let rest for 30 minutes or until you can gently poke the dough with one finger and the indentation slowly fills in about halfway. While the buns rest, preheat the oven to 325°F.

7. When the buns have finished their final proof, brush them with an egg wash and bake for 15 minutes, or until golden brown on top.

8. While the buns bake, prepare the syrup. In a medium-sized saucepot over high heat, combine sugar, water, and rum. Stir the mixture until the sugar dissolves, then let simmer for 5 minutes. Turn off the heat and let cool.

9. When the buns are finished baking and have cooled slightly (about 5 minutes), dunk them in the syrup. After dunking, place them back on the baking sheet. Brush each bun with honey, then sprinkle with walnuts. Enjoy the buns alongside a cup of coffee or tea, remembering the perseverance of these soldiers.

Eastertide

EASTER IS THE HIGHEST HOLIDAY FOR CHRISTIANS—the day we celebrate the resurrection of Jesus. In the week leading up to Easter, called Holy Week, we rehearse the final days of Jesus' life. First, we wave palms to commemorate Jesus' entrance into Jerusalem. In some churches, people share a meal and wash one another's feet on Maundy Thursday, remembering Jesus' Last Supper in the upper room with his disciples. On Good Friday, the altar is stripped, and congregants leave the church in silence. We know that Easter is coming, but just as Jesus wept over Lazarus's death, we grieve Jesus' death.

In my church's tradition, Easter begins with a vigil on Saturday night. We enter the church in darkness and silence, lit only by the paschal candle. We hear readings from Scripture that foretell what Jesus accomplished on the cross, each reading accompanied by a work of art—a song, a dance, a poem, or a visual installation. With each reading, the light grows a bit brighter until finally the priest shouts, "Alleluia, he is risen!" We ring bells and bang tambourines; we jingle keys and cry, "Alleluia!" in response.

Oh death, where is your victory? Oh grave, where is your sting? Jesus, our Lord, is risen indeed.

But Easter doesn't end on Easter Sunday. Like the season of Christmastide, Easter carries on much longer—fifty days, to be exact. For seven weeks, we continue to celebrate the resurrection of our Lord. I once attended a church that marked these seven weeks with a series of Eastertide feasts. The first took place after the Easter vigil, a dessert reception that carried on late into the night. After that we had dinner in the homes of church members every week, with almost a hundred people crowded into a small Boston flat, eating and laughing and celebrating the community formed through Christ.

Easter is also a celebration of the arrival of spring. It's a time bursting with life. After the great fast of Lent, Orthodox Christians and medieval Catholics would have had an abundance of eggs, as well as milk and butter, to use up. The eggs came in handy for Easter celebrations, as they were decorated and then hidden for children to find—reminiscent of the women searching for Jesus in the tomb. Almost every region where Christianity has thrived has its own unique form of Easter bread. Many of these recipes contain milk, butter, and eggs, using up the stores that would have been on hand. Many include decorated eggs nestled into the loaf as well.

Though Easter has not become quite as commercialized as Christmas, the focus on baskets and bunnies threatens to distract us from the true power of this day. In our Easter feasts and egg hunts, may we remember Christians throughout history who have used these activities to point toward Jesus' resurrection. He has overcome sin and death. Alleluia. Alleluia.

BREATH PRAYER
INHALE: *Alleluia, Christ is risen!*
EXHALE: *Risen indeed!*

COLLECT

Resurrected God,
you walked with your disciples
on the path to Emmaus,
talking, listening, laughing,
but known only in
the breaking of bread.

May we taste your goodness
as we feast today,
Bread of Life present with us.
Amen.

Hot Cross Buns

Good Friday (the Friday before Easter) | Difficulty Level: +++

Makes 12 buns

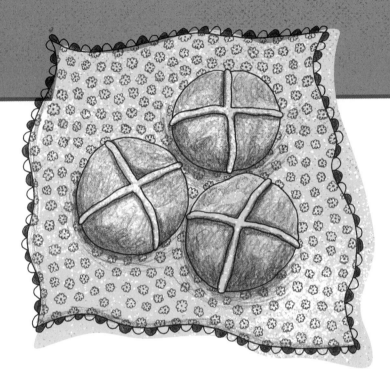

HOT CROSS BUNS ARE A GOOD FRIDAY TREAT with many myths and legends behind them. It's said that a bun baked on Good Friday will never go stale and that a bun shared between friends cements the friendship for the coming year. In medieval times, the buns were preserved for their healing qualities—grated and pressed into wounds or swallowed for rapid recovery.

Some bakers were said to incorporate crushed blessed Communion wafers into the dough, which is likely why the buns were believed to have healing qualities. But to use the consecrated bread in this way would have also been sacrilegious. To keep the blessed body of Christ from being used in this manner, in 1592 Queen Elizabeth I demanded that the serving of hot cross buns be limited to Good Friday, Christmas, and funerals.

The spices studding the rolls represent the spices that embalmed Christ at his burial, and the cross sliced across the top or piped on with icing represents the cross where he died.

While the exact provenance of hot cross buns is unknown, the most compelling claim comes from Saint Alban's Cathedral, where it's said the fourteenth-century monk Brother Thomas Rocliffe developed a recipe for buns made with the expensive spice grains of paradise, in the same family as cardamom. On Good Friday, Brother Thomas passed out the buns to the poor. Word of the delicious buns spread, and many bakers attempted to replicate them. But Saint Alban's claims the original recipe never left the safety of their walls. To this day, the bakers at Saint Alban's hold to this historic formula.

The name hot cross buns was first recorded in the year 1733, when *Poor Robin's Almanac* posted a well-known ditty sung by women walking the street to sell their spiced treats:

> *Good Friday comes this month,*
> *the old woman runs,*
> *with one a penny, two a penny*
> *hot cross buns.*

DOUGH

- 1 cup (8 ounces) milk
- 3 cups (12.75 ounces) all-purpose or bread flour
- 2 tablespoons granulated sugar
- 2 teaspoons instant yeast
- 1 teaspoon kosher salt
- 1/2 teaspoon cinnamon
- 1/4 teaspoon cardamom
- 1/4 teaspoon nutmeg
- 1/4 teaspoon allspice
- 1/4 teaspoon coriander
- 1 egg
- 4 tablespoons (2 ounces) unsalted butter, softened and cut into 1/4-inch cubes
- 1/3 cup (2.1 ounces) golden raisins
- 1/3 cup (2.1 ounces) dried cranberries

TOPPING

- Egg wash

ICING

- 2 cups (8 ounces) powdered sugar
- Zest and juice of 1 orange

---

1. Heat milk for 30 seconds in the microwave to remove the chill. You can also heat milk over the stove on low heat until just barely warm to the touch.

2. In a large bowl, combine flour, sugar, yeast, salt, and spices. Create a well in the center of the flour mixture. Pour the milk into the well, along with the egg.

3. Mix the ingredients with your hand until the flour is hydrated. You might have to squeeze the dough to help distribute the egg all the way through. Let the dough rest, covered, at room temperature for 15 minutes.

4. Knead the dough inside the bowl using a method similar to the stretch-and-fold technique described in part 2 of this book. It will be a bit sticky. Once the dough is manageable, you can turn it onto the counter to knead until

smooth and the dough passes the windowpane test. If it is too sticky to turn onto the counter, simply knead it in the bowl the entire time.

5. Once the dough is smooth, place it back in the bowl. Sprinkle the butter over the dough. Squeeze the butter into the dough and knead inside the bowl, using the stretch-and-fold method until the butter is melted and distributed into the dough. Add the dried fruit and knead just until the pieces are evenly distributed through the dough. Cover and let the dough rest at room temperature until doubled in size, about 1–1 1/2 hours.

6. Divide the dough into 12 even pieces, about 2.3 ounces each. Shape each piece into a round. Place the buns about 2 inches apart on a single baking sheet lined with parchment paper or a silicone mat. Cover with plastic wrap or a damp tea towel and let rest at room temperature for 45–60 minutes, until you can gently poke the dough with one finger and the indentation slowly fills in halfway. While the dough rests, preheat the oven to 325°F.

7. Just before putting the buns in the oven, brush them with egg wash. Bake for 15–20 minutes, until golden brown. Let cool.

8. After the buns have cooled, make the icing. In a medium-sized mixing bowl, combine the powdered sugar and orange zest. Add half of the juice from the orange. Stir until combined. Continue adding more juice as necessary, until the icing reaches a thick but smooth consistency.

9. Transfer the icing into a piping bag or a medium-sized plastic baggie. Snip the corner of the bag and pipe the icing into a cross shape on each bun.

Paska

Eastertide (the seven weeks after Easter) | Difficulty Level: ++++

PASKA IS A UKRAINIAN EASTER BREAD, similar in flavor and texture to an Italian panettone. It has a light texture, baked into a tall dome covered in icing and colorful sprinkles. The domes are said to look like the domes of a church. While I bake my paska in a panettone mold to achieve the tall dome, many bakers make theirs inside coffee cans.

Ukrainian paska is similar to Russian kulich, which is served with a cream cheese–like spread called paskha, suggesting similar origins to the breads. Mennonites in Canada make their own version of paska, an enriched bun or loaf of bread smeared with thick icing and sprinkles. Some Ukrainians and Ukrainian-Americans make a bread topped with elaborate braids rather than icing, similar to Serbian slavski kolac (see the Advent section).

As with hot cross buns, paska carries with it a number of mystical traditions. It's said that while the paska rises, the home must remain calm. If the dough falls or the bread collapses when emerging from the oven, it foretells a death in the family.

Paska is typically brought to church to be blessed by the priest before it is served at the Easter feast. Folklore says that if farmers bury crumbs of the blessed bread, they are sure to have a successful harvest.

DOUGH

- 1/4 cup (2 ounces) milk
- 2 1/2 cups (10.6 ounces) all-purpose or bread flour, divided
- 2 tablespoons + 2 teaspoons granulated sugar
- 1 1/2 teaspoons instant yeast
- 2 eggs
- 1/4 cup (2 ounces) sour cream
- 1 teaspoon kosher salt
- 4 tablespoons (2 ounces) unsalted butter, softened and cut into 1/4-inch cubes
- 1/2 cup (3.2 ounces) golden raisins

ICING

- 2 cups (8 ounces) powdered sugar
- 2 tablespoons lemon juice

TOPPING

Sprinkles, for decoration

---

1. Heat milk for 30 seconds in the microwave to remove the chill. You can also heat milk over the stove on low heat until just barely warm to the touch.

2. In a large bowl, mix 1 cup of the flour with granulated sugar and yeast, then add milk, eggs, and sour cream. Stir until smooth and let rest for 30 minutes.

3. Add the rest of the flour and the salt to the dough, kneading the dough inside the bowl until it's smooth. Let rest for 15 minutes.

4. Add the butter to the dough, squeezing the dough to distribute the butter all the way through. Sprinkle the raisins over the top of the dough, then knead

the dough inside the bowl using a method similar to the stretch-and-fold technique described in part 2 of this book. It will be very sticky.

5. Once the dough is smooth and no pockets of butter remain, cover the dough and let it rise until doubled in size, about 1 hour.

6. Spray either a panettone mold, a 6-inch-tall cake pan, or a coffee can with pan spray, then pour the dough inside. Cover and let rise again until doubled in size, about 1 hour. While the dough rises, preheat the oven to 350°F.

7. Bake the bread for 45 minutes, then let cool. While the bread cools, mix the powdered sugar and lemon juice to make an icing. After the bread has cooled, pour the icing over the top and decorate with colorful sprinkles. Slice and serve. (A priest's blessings, optional.)

Pinca

Eastertide (the seven weeks after Easter) | Difficulty Level: +++

PINCA IS A SWEET CROATIAN EASTER BREAD made yellow by an abundance of egg yolks.

Pinca is also known as sirnica in the region of Dalmatia and jajara in the region of Zagorje. The name sirnica means "cheesecake," suggesting that this bread was originally made with curdled dairy to help it rise instead of yeast.

The pinca dough is made into a round, then it's decorated with a three-pronged star slashed across the top. Sometimes the dough is braided into a round using a three-strand braid. In both cases, the use of three slashes or three strands is said to signify the three persons of the Trinity. The wreath shape is meant to look like Jesus' crown of thorns. This loaf is added to an Easter picnic basket that is brought to the church on Easter morning for a blessing.

Extra pinca dough gets shaped into dolls called primorski uskrsne bebe, which means "Easter babies from Primorje," the region from which the tradition hails. These dolls are made with a braided dough body encasing a dyed egg as the face and then given to children.

This technique of decorating Easter bread with an egg is mirrored across Europe in Easter breads from different regions: Greek tsoureki, Italian pane di pasqua, Armenian choreg, Bulgarian kozunak, Spanish mondes de pascua (which includes sprinkles, much like the Ukrainian paska), and Portuguese massa sovada. The biggest variance between these breads is the type of spices used to flavor the dough.

The recipe below is for the loaf that gets added to the Easter basket, but if you have extra dough, you might enjoy shaping it into an Easter doll. Don't forget to add a dyed egg as the face!

DOUGH

1/2	cup (4 ounces) milk
2 1/2	cups (10.6 ounces) all-purpose or bread flour
2	tablespoons + 2 teaspoons granulated sugar
1 1/2	teaspoons instant yeast
1	teaspoon kosher salt
	Zest of 1 lemon and 1 orange
1	tablespoon (1/2 ounce) rum
1	egg + 1 egg yolk
4	tablespoons (2 ounces) unsalted butter, softened and cubed

TOPPING

Egg wash

Hard-boiled, dyed egg (optional)

1. Heat milk for 30 seconds in the microwave to remove the chill. You can also heat milk over the stove on low heat until just barely warm to the touch.

2. In a large bowl, combine the flour, sugar, yeast, salt, and citrus zest. Form a small well in the center of the flour mixture. Pour the milk, rum, and eggs into the well.

3. Mix the ingredients with your hand until the flour is hydrated.

4. Knead the dough inside the bowl using a method similar to the stretch-and-fold technique described in part 2 of this book.

5. Once the gluten has begun to form, mix in the butter. Squeeze the dough to help distribute the butter all the way through. It will be very sticky. Let the dough rest for 15 minutes.

6. After the dough has had a 15-minute rest, stretch and fold the dough 16–20 times. Cover and let rest at room temperature until doubled in size, about 1–1 1/2 hours.

7. Once the dough has risen, shape it into a round. Place on a baking tray, cover, and let rise at room temperature until you can gently poke the dough with one finger and the indentation slowly fills in halfway. While the dough rests, preheat the oven to 325°F.

8. Just before putting the loaf in the oven, brush it with egg wash, then slice with three slashes in the shape of a star to symbolize the Trinity. Bake for 25–30 minutes, until golden brown. Let cool. (Additional dough baby, optional.)

Defo Dabo

Eastertide (the seven weeks after Easter) | Difficulty Level: ++

DEFO DABO IS AN ETHIOPIAN RAISED BREAD that is wrapped in enset (false banana leaves) during baking, typically in a pot covered in embers underground.

The kinds of raised breads we've made so far in this book require wheat with strong gluten structure and the use of an oven. In regions that do not typically use ovens or that do not grow high-gluten wheat, breads often take different forms, such as flatbreads baked on top of a heat source, or fry breads baked in hot oil.

The bread most often associated with Ethiopia is injera, a flatbread made from a fermented grain called teff. However, thanks to Ethiopia's historical ties to Judaism, a number of raised-bread techniques have been developed there as well. In Jewish practice, bread is required for the Shabbat dinner, and Ethiopian Jews didn't consider injera proper bread for this occasion.

While Ethiopia does grow strong wheat, they don't have a tradition of baking in ovens, so creative baking methods, such as loaves wrapped in leaves and buried underground, were required. The leaves lend smokiness to the bread, which pairs well with the spices in it—especially the coriander and nigella seeds, meant to parallel the manna in the wilderness.

The dough is a high-hydration dough, like the loaf we made in the first half of this book. It can be baked in a cake pan or a Dutch oven, as with that recipe, but wrapped in enset (if you can find it) or parchment paper, foil, lettuce, or banana leaves.

Christianity arrived in Ethiopia early, with the baptism of the Ethiopian eunuch recounted in the book of Acts, before spreading across North Africa. This raised bread is commonly served among Ethiopian Christians on Easter, known as Fasika in the Ethiopian Orthodox Church.

DOUGH

2 1/2 cups (10.6 ounces) all-purpose
       or bread flour

2   teaspoons instant yeast

1   teaspoon granulated sugar

1   teaspoon kosher salt

1   teaspoon nigella seeds

1/2 teaspoon ground coriander

3/4 cup (6 ounces) water, just
    warm to the touch

1   tablespoon neutral oil,
    such as avocado, sunflower,
    or canola oil

FOR BAKING

Enset or banana leaves

1. In a medium-sized mixing bowl, combine flour, yeast, sugar, salt, nigella seeds, and coriander. Form a well in the center of the flour mixture and add the water and oil.

2. Mix the flour and water, then knead for 6–8 minutes in the bowl or on the counter. When the dough is smooth and passes the windowpane test, place it back in the bowl, cover, and let rise at room temperature until doubled in size, about 45 minutes.

3. While the dough rests, line the bottom and sides of an 8-inch cake pan or a Dutch oven with enset or banana leaves. If you can't find enset or banana leaves, parchment paper or large leaves of lettuce will do.

4. When the dough has doubled in size, shape it into a round, then place over the leaves. Put a layer of leaves on top as well.

5. Let the dough rise for 15–20 more minutes, until you can gently poke the dough with one finger and the indentation slowly fills in halfway. While the dough rests, preheat the oven to 325°F.

6. Bake for 30 minutes. Remove the leaves, let cool, slice, and enjoy.

All Saints Day

THE CELEBRATION OF ALL SAINTS DATES BACK to the eighth century, when Pope Gregory IV established All Saints or Hallowmas as a holiday on the church calendar—a day to honor the many saints whose feast days weren't fixed.

For many people around the world, November 1 and 2 were days that marked the coming of winter and the shortening of days. Winter is a season of death—the death of crops and trees, a reminder of the never-ending cycle of life. As such, the shifting of the seasons was a time to honor those who had passed away by lighting the night sky with fire.

When Pope Gregory wanted a day set aside to mark the saints who had passed away, November 1 made sense, as it replaced the pagan traditions in nearby countries. The holiday began, like Christmas and Easter, with a service the evening before. This was called Hallowmas Eve, or Hallowmas E'en—Halloween, as we know it now. November 2 became a day to honor all loved ones who had passed away, including those who had not received the reverential status of saint. It was called All Souls' Day.

Christians have long marked the reality of death through artistic symbols, or memento mori, which translates to "remember your death." As we are reminded each Ash Wednesday, it is from dust we came and to dust we will return. The temporal nature of our earthly lives reminds us that we also exist in a global and historical communion of saints—the family of God that is not bound by the limits of time or space. In the tension between our temporality and God's eternity, some Christians honor and pray for the dead who are now in the presence of God and ask that these brothers and sisters in Christ intercede for us here on earth as well.

Some medieval churches marked All Souls with a parade of relics—items associated with particular saints, such as a piece of a veil said to belong to Mary or a splinter said to have come from the cross where Jesus died. Those who were too poor to pay for access to relics would dress up instead—not as ghosts or witches, but as their favorite saints.

While these practices offered methods for the poor to participate creatively in the holiday, there was no doubt a good deal of corruption intertwined in these church practices. According to the church's teachings on purgatory, a loved one's liminal time could be shortened through prayers and indulgences. Initially, an indulgence required a series of penitential acts, including prayers, confessions, and the viewing of relics. It was a means of recognizing the punishment of sin that Christ had already forgiven. But by 1517, the focus had shifted to a monetary payment to the church, the funds going toward the rebuilding of Saint Peter's Church in Rome.

Horrified by this corrupt practice that preyed on faithful Christians, Martin Luther chose Halloween as the day to nail his ninety-five theses to the door of the Wittenberg Church—a common destination for pilgrims on All Saints.

Like the festival of Carnival or Fat Tuesday, Halloween is a ritual of subversion. The shifting of seasons creates a liminal space where norms are suspended for a short time. The subversion of norms helps to reveal deeper truths about the way things are. Martin Luther played into this practice of subversion when he nailed his theses to the door.

Perhaps the evil you fear, he warned, is coming from *inside* the church. Perhaps your corruption dishonors the faithful saints who have gone before.

Regardless of how you feel about participating in the festivities around

Halloween, All Saints, All Souls, or the Day of the Dead, I hope these recipes serve as a reminder that we are part of a community far beyond ourselves. The bread that unites us to Christ unites us also to Christ's body, a community of people unbound by the limits of space or time.

BREATH PRAYER
INHALE: *Oh death,*
EXHALE: *where is your sting?*

COLLECT
God who is behind and before all things,
you are not bound by the limits of space or time.
Yet you called each of us to the time and place
in which we were born.

In every bite of bread, remind us that we
are inextricably linked to those who've gone before
and those who will reside in your world after we are gone.

Protect us from the powers and principalities
of greed, of violence, of polarization
that harm and divide your beloved creation.

Make us instead
instruments of peace,
passing down your love to the next generation.
Amen.

Soul Cakes

Feast of All Saints and All Souls (October 31–November 2) | Difficulty Level: +

Makes 16–20 cakes

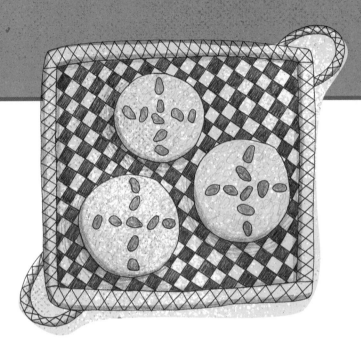

THROUGHOUT THE EARLY MIDDLE AGES, Britain's poor would go from door to door on Halloween, offering prayers of intercession for each household's deceased. In exchange, they would receive a cake marked with the sign of a cross—a soul cake, as it was called. They'd sing,

> *Soul! Soul! For a soul cake!*
> *I pray good mistress for a soul cake! . . .*
> *One for Peter, two for Paul,*
> *Three for him who made us all.*

Up with the kettle and down with the pan,
Give us good alms and we'll be gone.

In time, the practice became known as "souling," the precursor to modern-day trick-or-treating.

These soul cakes are more like a soft, not-too-sweet cookie than what we might call a cake today, but whether you consider them cookies, cakes, or breads, they are a delicious way to remember and thank God for your own departed loved ones.

8   tablespoons (4 ounces)
    unsalted butter, softened and
    cut into 1/4-inch cubes

1/2 cup (3.6 ounces) granulated
     sugar

2   egg yolks

2   cups (8.5 ounces) all-purpose
    or bread flour

1/2 teaspoon cinnamon

1/4 teaspoon turmeric

1/4 teaspoon nutmeg

1/4 teaspoon ginger

1/4 teaspoon coriander

1/4 teaspoon allspice

1/4 teaspoon kosher salt

2   tablespoons milk

TOPPING

Egg wash

1/4 cup (1.7 ounces) golden raisins

1. In a medium-sized mixing bowl, mix butter and sugar until thoroughly combined. Add egg yolks and mix until fully incorporated.

2. In a small mixing bowl, sift together flour, spices, and salt.

3. Fold flour mixture into the butter mixture. Add the milk when the flour is almost fully combined. Mix just until the ingredients are fully incorporated and the dough is smooth. It should feel like a sugar cookie dough. The goal is not to build up gluten in this recipe, so be careful not to overmix.

4. Let the dough rest in the refrigerator for 30 minutes to chill.

5. After the dough has rested, preheat the oven to 325°F. Roll the dough onto a lightly floured kitchen counter to 1/4-inch thickness.

6. Using a 4-inch circular cookie cutter or the lid of a wide-mouthed mason jar, cut as many circles as you can out of the dough. Gently knead the scraps back together, roll out, and cut again. You should get about 16–20 circles out of this recipe.

7. Place the cakes on two baking sheets, 8–10 on each. Brush each cake with egg wash, then place golden raisins on the cakes in the shape of a cross.

8. Bake the cakes for 10 minutes, let cool, and enjoy. I like to serve these to the friends who come over to help me pass out candy to the neighborhood children.

Pão de Deus

Feast of All Saints and All Souls (October 31–November 2) | Difficulty Level: +++

Makes 12 buns

SIMILAR TO THE MEDIEVAL BRITISH PRACTICE of souling and the modern American practice of trick-or-treating, Portuguese children spend the morning of November 1 traveling door to door asking, "Pão por Deus?" which means "Bread for God?"

As with souling, this practice began with the poor asking for food and eventually became an activity for children. They receive pão de Deus in exchange—a sweet bun topped with caramelized coconut that tastes like it truly could be bread from heaven.

Portuguese cuisine is heavily influenced by its Moorish history as well as the places it colonized, featuring lots of spices as well as ingredients acquired in the New World. The coconut and rum in pão de Deus are two such examples.

Pão de Deus are not limited to All Saints' Day. They are also eaten alongside coffee for breakfast all year round, although they are most commonly associated with this holiday.

DOUGH

3/4 cup (6 ounces) whole milk

3 cups (12.75 ounces) all-purpose or bread flour

2 tablespoons granulated sugar

2 teaspoons instant yeast

1 teaspoon kosher salt

2 tablespoons (1 ounce) rum

1 egg

4 tablespoons (2 ounces) unsalted butter, softened and cut into 1/4-inch cubes

TOPPING

1 cup (2.6 ounces) unsweetened coconut flakes

2 tablespoons granulated sugar

1/2 egg, beaten and divided

1. Heat milk for 30 seconds in the microwave to remove the chill. You can also heat milk over the stove on low heat until just barely warm to the touch.

2. In a large bowl, combine flour, sugar, yeast, and salt. Create a well in the center of the flour mixture. Pour the milk and rum into the well. In a separate bowl, beat the egg with a fork. Mix half the egg mixture (about 1 1/2 tablespoons, or 1 ounce) with the milk and rum.

3. Mix the ingredients with your hand until the flour is hydrated. Let the dough rest, covered, at room temperature for 15 minutes.

4. Knead the dough inside the bowl using a method similar to the stretch-and-fold technique described in part 2 of this book. It will be a bit sticky. Once the dough is manageable, you can turn it onto the counter to knead until the dough is smooth and passes the windowpane test. If it's too sticky to turn onto the counter, simply knead it in the bowl the entire time.

5. Once the dough is smooth, place the dough back in the bowl. Sprinkle the butter over the dough. You might have to squeeze the dough to help distribute the butter all the way.

6. Cover and let the dough rest at room temperature until doubled in size, about 1–1 1/2 hours. If your kitchen is warm or humid, you can rest the dough in the refrigerator for half the time to prevent stickiness.

7. Divide the dough into 12 even pieces, about 2–2.2 ounces each. Shape each piece into a round. If the dough is sticky, use a tiny bit of flour to prevent the dough from sticking to your hands while you shape. Place the buns on a single baking sheet lined with parchment paper or a silicone mat.

8. In a medium-sized mixing bowl, combine the coconut flakes, the remaining sugar, and the 1/2 egg. (Beat the egg lightly before adding half to the coconut-sugar mixture.) Spoon the mixture over the top of each bun.

9. Cover with plastic wrap or a damp tea towel and let rest at room temperature for 45 minutes to an hour, until you can gently poke the dough with one finger and the indentation slowly fills in halfway. While the dough rests, preheat the oven to 325°F.

10. Bake for 20–25 minutes, until golden brown. Let cool and serve alongside a mug of coffee, hot chocolate, milk, or tea.

Guaguas de Pan

Feast of All Saints and All Souls (October 31–November 2) | Difficulty Level: +++
Makes 12 buns

GUAGUAS DE PAN, WHICH TRANSLATES TO "BREAD BABIES," are an All Saints treat from Ecuador. These breads are shaped to look like a doll and given as gifts from godparents to their godchildren on All Souls' Day, or Dia de los Difuntos ("Day of the Deceased"), in Ecuador. The bread, made with an enriched dough like a brioche, is similar to the Mexican pan de muerto, which is also popular at this time of year.

The breads are decorated with colorful icing to look like a child and served alongside colada morada, a drink made of blue corn, fruit, and spices. Some breads are made not for eating but for placing on the graves of loved ones, where it dries out and lasts for weeks or longer. Some say the reason for decorating the buns like babies is to reflect the innocence that humans return to after death. Others say it is reminiscent of ancient mummies.

As we learned with the concha recipe, wheat is not indigenous to the Americas. It was introduced by the Spanish in the sixteenth century. The bread culture in Ecuador developed separately from that in Mexico, though it was similarly inspired by the presence of French bakers.

While most Ecuadorians were slow to develop a taste for wheat (it was mostly produced for the colonizers who wanted European-style loaves), an indigenous bread made with a mix of white corn, quinoa, and yucca flours is said to have a flavor and texture similar to fine French breads made with wheat. This bread is still made by Ecuadorian bakers today.

Both indigenous and European-style breads in Ecuador were leavened using the leftovers from chicha, a fermented drink related to colada morada. The process was likely similar to baking with barm, the leftovers from the beer-brewing process, which was common in most of the world. Today bakers typically use commercial yeast.

DOUGH

- 1 cup (8 ounces) milk
- 5 cups (1 pound, 5.25 ounces) all-purpose or bread flour
- 1/2 cup (3.6 ounces) granulated sugar
- 1 tablespoon instant yeast
- 2 teaspoons kosher salt
- 2 teaspoons cinnamon
- Zest of 2 oranges
- 2 eggs
- 8 tablespoons (4 ounces) unsalted butter, softened and cut into 1/4-inch cubes
- 2 teaspoons orange blossom water

FILLING

- 1/2–1 cup (4–8 ounces) dulce de leche
- 1/2–1 cup (6–12 ounces) guava paste

TOPPING

- Egg wash

ICING

- 1 cup (4 ounces) powdered sugar
- 2 tablespoons heavy cream
- Food coloring

1. Heat milk for 30 seconds in the microwave to remove the chill. You can also heat milk over the stove on low heat until just barely warm to the touch.

2. In a large bowl, mix flour, sugar, yeast, salt, cinnamon, and orange zest.

3. Form a well in the middle of the flour mixture and add the milk, eggs, butter, and orange blossom water.

4. Mix the ingredients with your hand until the flour is hydrated. You might have to squeeze the dough to help distribute the butter all the way through. Knead the dough inside the bowl using a method similar to the stretch-and-fold technique described in part 2 of this book. It will be sticky. Once the dough is manageable, you can turn it onto the counter to knead until the dough is smooth and passes the windowpane test. If the dough is very sticky, you can add a bit more flour as you knead.

5. Once the dough is smooth, place the dough back in the bowl. Cover and let the dough rest at room temperature until doubled in size, about 1–1 1/2 hours.

6. Divide the dough into 12 pieces (about 3.2–3.4 ounces each) and press into ovals about 3 inches by 6 inches. Place either 1 heaping tablespoon of dulce de leche or 1 ounce of guava paste about one-third of the way from the bottom, then fold the bottom third up over the middle third to seal in the filling. Press the dough together to make sure the filling is sealed in tightly. (If it's not tightly sealed, the filling will ooze out.) Then roll up the final third. Press the seam once more, then squeeze gently about one-third of the way from the top to create a small head. If you'd like, you can use little pieces of dough to create eyes for the dolls.

7. Cover the buns and let rise at room temperature about 20–25 minutes, until you can gently poke the dough with one finger and the indentation slowly filles in halfway. While the buns rise, preheat the oven to 325°F.

8. When the buns are ready for the oven, brush them with the egg wash, then bake for 25–30 minutes, until golden brown on top. Let cool.

9. While the buns are cooling, mix up the icing. Combine the powdered sugar and cream until smooth. Divide into 3–4 smaller bowls and add a different food coloring to each. When the buns are cool, drizzle the icing on the bottom portion of each bun to look like a swaddled baby. Let the icing harden, then enjoy!

PART 5

PRAYERS FOR
EVERY OCCASION

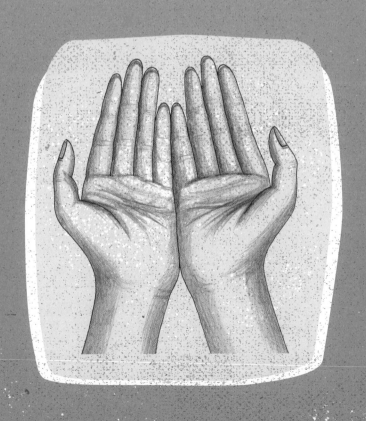

I'VE ALWAYS BEEN EQUAL PARTS INSPIRED AND INTIMIDATED by the invitation to pray without ceasing. As beautiful as it sounds to be in constant communication with God, in practice it has often felt impractical to me. In the ebb and flow of days that feel busy or simply mundane, I often find it difficult to pray.

When I learned that even the movements of my body could be offered to God as prayer, I began to see how praying without ceasing doesn't mean I have to have words for God at all times. It means I can simply walk through my days attuned to God's presence with me in every moment. At the same time, praying through these movements helped me find words to pray in these mundane moments as well.

Part 4 of this book includes breath prayers and collects to help you bake as a form of prayer during each liturgical season. But I want you to feel equipped to bake as a form of prayer throughout the year, no matter the purpose of your bake.

The breath prayers and collects in this section are designed to fit whatever circumstance you're baking for—whether for Communion, for a dinner with friends, to welcome a new neighbor, or in a season of grief. The goal of this section is to help you bake as a form of prayer during Ordinary Time as a reminder of the ways God is present not only amid holy days but in the mundane moments of every day as well.

As with the previous breath prayers and collects, these can be inserted into the Liturgy for Bread Baking found in part 3 of this book. They can be used when baking all kinds of recipes, whether they're recipes from this book or your favorite family recipes.

I hope these liturgies, prayers, and recipes will serve as tools to deepen your worship of God and deepen your connection to God's people throughout history and around the world.

BAKING FOR A DINNER WITH FRIENDS

BREATH PRAYER

INHALE: *Show hospitality to one another*

EXHALE: *as good stewards of God's varied grace.*

1 Peter 4:9-10

COLLECT

Hospitable God,
thank you for building
your church around the table:
a reminder of our need for others.

You delight in the ways
we are transformed through
relationships with friends.
May this bread build bonds
between those who eat it,
deepening both trust and joy.
Amen.

BAKING FOR A DINNER WITH FAMILY

BREATH PRAYER

INHALE: *Let every person be quick to hear,*
EXHALE: *slow to speak, and slow to anger.*
James 1:19

COLLECT
Jesus, Son of Mary,
brother of James, Joseph,
Simon, Jude, and unnamed sisters,
What were your family dinners like?

Did you all keep one another laughing?
Or did you bicker about who got
the last bite of bread?

May our family find joy in conversation
with one another, or at least in delicious food,
even when our differences remain.
Amen.

BAKING FOR A FAMILY WITH A NEW BABY

BREATH PRAYER

INHALE: *You knit me together*

EXHALE: *in my mother's womb.*

Psalm 139:13

COLLECT

Creator God,
you know both the joy
and the exhaustion
a new child can bring.

You hear the cries of parents
overcome with love, weariness, and fear.
You hear their prayers as they rock and dream
about who this child will be.

May this bread be a small reminder
of your presence with those who eat it,
a balm in the midst of long, sleepless nights.
Amen.

BAKING FOR A NEW NEIGHBOR

INHALE: *Love your neighbor*
EXHALE: *as yourself.*
Mark 12:31

COLLECT
Wandering Jesus,
the Gospels tell us that
you had no place
to lay your head.

You know quite well the
excitement and trepidation
of being somewhere new.

May this bread be an invitation
for my new neighbor
to feel at home in this place.
Amen.

BAKING FOR SOMEONE WHO IS GRIEVING

BREATH PRAYER

INHALE: *The Lord is close to the brokenhearted*

EXHALE: *and saves those who are crushed in spirit.*

Psalm 34:18

COLLECT

God who wept,
you know the ache of grief,
the knots in the stomach,
and the pain that permeates to the bone.

You say that one day you will wipe away
every tear from every eye.
But today is not that day.

Be with my friend in their grief.
May your Spirit comfort them as they weep,
and may this bread nourish them along the way.
Amen.

BAKING FOR A WEDDING

INHALE: *What God has joined together,*

EXHALE: *let no one separate.*

Matthew 19:6

COLLECT

God who performed your first miracle
at a wedding in Cana,
you delight in the covenant of marriage.

You say it mirrors
the holy mystery
of Christ and his Church.

Let this bread serve as a
tangible reminder of your presence
in this celebration.

May this marriage be marked by
joy, comfort, and a continuation
of the hospitality shown today.
Amen.

BAKING FOR A BIRTHDAY

BREATH PRAYER

INHALE: *Teach us to number our days,*

EXHALE: *that we might grow in wisdom.*

Psalm 90:12

COLLECT

God who ordains each day of our lives
before one of them comes to be,
you created [name] in your image,
out of an abundance
of love and joy.

I am grateful to know you
more fully through
my relationship with them.

Bless the coming year for this dear friend.
May they know you more fully and more fully reflect
the abundance of your love.
Amen.

BAKING COMMUNION BREAD

INHALE: *This is my body,*
EXHALE: *broken for you.*
1 Corinthians 11:24

COLLECT
O Bread of Life,
the night before your death,
you offered a meal
to your disciples.

You fed bread to the ones
you loved, and even
to the one who would betray.

Be with me as I bake this loaf
for those I love (and for those who are a struggle).
May this bread bind us together
and make us more like you.
Amen.

BAKING FOR A LOVE FEAST[1]

BREATH PRAYER

INHALE: *They devoted themselves to fellowship,*

EXHALE: *to the breaking of bread and to prayer.*

Acts 2:42

COLLECT

God of community,
you created us to know you
through the community of your Church:
a Church established around the table.

As we gather over bread,
remembering the meals of our spiritual ancestors,
members of the early church described in Acts,
may we worship you wholeheartedly
and love one another fully,
formed by the breaking of bread and prayer.
Amen.

---

[1] For more about Love Feasts, see the Moravian Sugar Cake recipe under "Christmastide" in part 4.

BAKING FOR A CHURCH POTLUCK

INHALE: *Eat your food with gladness,*
EXHALE: *and drink your wine with a joyful heart.*
Ecclesiastes 9:7

COLLECT
Creative God,
thank you for gifting us
with tongues and tastebuds,
with the ability to enjoy an abundance of foods.

Thank you for creating
each member of our church
with unique skills, in and out of the kitchen.

May this bread be a humble offering
to the church potluck spread.
And may the table be marked not by competition
but by an outpouring of joy.
Amen.

BAKING FOR A FUNERAL

BREATH PRAYER

INHALE: *Precious in the sight of the Lord*

EXHALE: *is the death of his faithful servants.*

Psalm 116:15

COLLECT

God of resurrection,
you are the God
who wept
at the death of your friend.

Like you, we weep too,
even as we know that
death is not the end.

May this bread be a comfort
in our present mourning
and a reminder of the life to come.
Amen.

BAKING THROUGH GRIEF

BREATH PRAYER

INHALE: *Cast your cares on the Lord*

EXHALE: *and the Lord will sustain you.*

Psalm 55:22

COLLECT

God who holds the grieving in your arms,
hold me today.
My body aches with grief,
and I wonder how I will
go on.

As I prepare this dough,
may I sense your love
all the way through my fingertips.

May the kneading and shaping
be a channel for my sorrow,
and may the eating be a comfort too.
Amen.

BAKING THROUGH DOUBT

INHALE: *I will strengthen you and help you;*
EXHALE: *I will uphold you.*
Isaiah 41:10

COLLECT

God,
I'm not so sure I know
what I believe anymore.
My certainty has turned to doubt.

I want to say, like the father in Scripture,
"I believe; help my unbelief!"
But I don't know what I believe anymore.

Be with me in my doubting;
reassure me of your steadfast love.
May I at least know you in this tangible way,
in this bread that I bake.
Amen.

BAKING THROUGH ANXIETY

BREATH PRAYER

INHALE: *When anxiety was great within me,*

EXHALE: *your consolation brought me joy.*

Psalm 94:19

COLLECT

God of peace,
you say that we should cast
all our fears upon you.
You say not to worry about a thing.

You say you will provide
even more than you do for the birds,
but I struggle to believe it's true.

My mind races endlessly,
and I don't know what comes next.
Be my comfort in the rhythms of this bake.
Amen.

BAKING WHEN DISCERNING NEXT STEPS

BREATH PRAYER

INHALE: *Trust in the Lord with all your heart;*

EXHALE: *the Lord will make your paths straight.*

Proverbs 3:5-6

COLLECT

God of discernment,
you knew each one of my days
before one of them came to pass.
You know my future even though I'm confused.

As I question what lies
on the path ahead,
assure me you are with me along the way.

Protect me from poor decisions,
and perhaps gently nudge me
in the direction I ought to go.
Amen.

BAKING IN CELEBRATION

BREATH PRAYER

INHALE: *The Lord has done great things for us,*
EXHALE: *and we are filled with joy.*
　　　　Psalm 126:3

COLLECT

God, you delight
when your creation celebrates.
You find joy in our joy.

You tell us to come before you
in thanksgiving, shouting our gladness.
And so I come before you today.

May my excitement spread
through each motion of this bake,
celebration bubbling over into each bite of the bread.
Amen.

BAKING WHEN LONELY

BREATH PRAYER
INHALE: *You find families*
EXHALE: *for those who are lonely.*
            Psalm 68:6

COLLECT
Triune God,
you say that
it is not good
for a human to be alone.

You tell us that you find families
for those who are lonely.
But I feel the sting of isolation today.

With each turn of this bread,
I beg you to
meet me in this need.

Ease my ache, and bring me
friends and family
to carry me through.
Amen.

BAKING WITH CHILDREN

BREATH PRAYER *(to be prayed silently as the children knead)*
INHALE: *Unless you become like children,*
EXHALE: *you will never enter the Kingdom of heaven.*
      Matthew 18:3

COLLECT
God,
you love these children
even more than I can understand—
and I love them so much my heart might burst.

And yet the mess on the counters,
on their faces, on their clothes
makes me wonder if this activity is worth it.

Give me patience, calm my worries,
relieve me from the feeling that
I should have done this by myself.

May their laughter bring me joy.
Amen.

BAKING IN A NEW HOUSE FOR THE FIRST TIME

BREATH PRAYER

INHALE: *By wisdom a house is built,*
EXHALE: *by understanding it is established.*
Proverbs 24:3

COLLECT

God, you created us
to long for grounding, for home.
Thank you for this place I now live.

You say that you stand at the door and knock,
that you will come in and eat with those
who hear your voice and open their home.

May I hear your voice in every knock
that comes on my door—
from neighbors, strangers, and friends.

Make this home a place marked
by gracious hospitality.
Amen.

BAKING IN A BELOVED KITCHEN FOR THE LAST TIME

BREATH PRAYER

INHALE: *Peace be with this house*

EXHALE: *and all who will live in here.*

Luke 10:5

COLLECT

God who left your dwelling place
to make a home on earth,
you know the pain of leaving.
You wandered with no place
to rest your head.

Be with me as I leave
this place I've come to love,
this kitchen that has brought me joy.

And be with those who will move in
and create a home here too.
Bring peace and joy at every meal they share.
Amen.

BAKING WHEN IT'S COLD OUTSIDE

BREATH PRAYER

INHALE: *The Lord bless you and keep you;*

EXHALE: *the Lord make his face shine upon you.*
Numbers 6:24-25

COLLECT

God of love,
you say that you go before us
as an all-consuming fire,
a holy love that purifies all in sight.

May I remember this fire
as the oven warms my home
and this bread warms my body,
from the inside out.
Amen.

BAKING AFTER A BAD DAY AT WORK

BREATH PRAYER

INHALE: *Those who know your name*

EXHALE: *put their trust in you.*

Psalm 9:10

COLLECT

God of peace,
I feel anything but peace today.
I'm riled up from everything
that seems to be going wrong.

Help me calm my breathing,
slow my body, ease my mind
with each turn of this dough.

You do not forsake
those who seek you.
Soothe me as I seek you today.
Amen.

BAKING A NEW RECIPE

BREATH PRAYER

INHALE: *The steadfast love of the Lord never ceases;*

EXHALE: *God's mercies are new every morning.*
Lamentations 3:22-23

COLLECT

God whose mercies are new every morning,
I am excited to also
embark on something new,
even as I worry I might fail.

Humble me as I mix and bake,
as I wonder how this dough will turn out.
Whether successful or not, the process is still good.

Help me find joy
in this current moment of unknown
and to find delight in whatever is to come.
Amen.

BAKING WHEN YOU NEED TO GET OUT OF YOUR HEAD

BREATH PRAYER

INHALE: *Be anxious about nothing;*

EXHALE: *the peace of God will guard your heart and mind.*
Philippians 4:6-7

COLLECT

God, my mind is spinning,
running on a loop,
and I don't know how to make it stop.
Help me focus on the feel of flour
sifting between my fingers—
a reminder of my sense of touch.

Help me smell the sweetness of
the dough in this bowl—
a reminder of the gift of my nose.

Help me savor the flavor of this bread,
after this long, slow bake—
a reminder that you are with me
in a tangible, tastable form.

You are my peace.
Amen.

BAKING WHEN YOU NEED TO SLOW DOWN

BREATH PRAYER

INHALE: *Sabbath was made for human beings,*

EXHALE: *not humans for the Sabbath.*

        Mark 2:27

COLLECT

God of rest,
you created for six days,
then on the last
you found delight in rest.

You command your followers
to rest like you—
a gift in our harried lives.

While I'm prone to keep pushing on,
I know this pace is bad for me.
Slow me down, Lord, body and mind,
That I might find rest in you.
Amen.

Conclusion

GOODNESS, ISN'T BREAD AMAZING?

I hope that as you reach the end of this book, you share with me the overwhelming recognition that Jesus' statement "I am the bread of Life" is no simple metaphor. It is a statement pregnant with life and meaning. I pray that each time you bake, you will grow in relationship with God and in understanding of God's beauty and presence.

I also hope that you are bursting with excitement over the prospect of praying through the physical movements of baking, breaking, and eating bread. Perhaps this practice has helped you consider other ways to pray with your body: through gardening, walking, dancing, and more.

But most of all, I hope this book has helped you delight in the diversity of the Christian faith as a global and historical community. It is a faith that has been practiced for thousands of years, in myriad ways, by millions of people all around the world.

It's a faith centered on a God who offers himself to us in the form of bread, a God we can know on our tongues and in our bellies, a God who promises us that despite our conflicts and our pain, we are still made one through this bread we share. Even amid the tension of our differences, we can see the beauty of God all the more.

I pray that as you bake and pray throughout the year, for all kinds of occasions, you will rest in the power of this truth.

Journaling Pages

THE FOLLOWING JOURNALING PAGES are designed to help you pay attention to the changes in your loaf, and in yourself, as you bake each loaf of bread. Use them along with the six lessons in this book, or anytime you want to pay attention to the rhythms of your dough.

Date:

Kitchen temperature: Start time:

Outside temperature: Shape time:

Water temperature: Bake time:

Humidity level: Length of bulk fermentation:

Describe how you feel as you begin baking your bread today:

_____

_____

What prayers, petitions, or thanksgivings are you bringing to God today?

_____

_____

_____

Describe how your dough looks and feels after your initial mix:

_____

_____

Describe how your dough looks and feels after the bulk fermentation:

_____

_____

Describe how your dough looks and feels during shaping:

_____

_____

Describe how your dough looks, feels, and tastes after baking and cooling:

_____

_____

How has God been present with you during today's bake?

_____

_____

_____

Date:

Kitchen temperature: Start time:

Outside temperature: Shape time:

Water temperature: Bake time:

Humidity level: Length of bulk fermentation:

Describe how you feel as you begin baking your bread today:

_____

_____

What prayers, petitions, or thanksgivings are you bringing to God today?

_____

_____

_____

Describe how your dough looks and feels after your initial mix:

_____

_____

Describe how your dough looks and feels after the bulk fermentation:

_____

_____

Describe how your dough looks and feels during shaping:

_____

_____

Describe how your dough looks, feels, and tastes after baking and cooling:

_____

_____

How has God been present with you during today's bake?

_____

_____

_____

Date:

Kitchen temperature: Start time:

Outside temperature: Shape time:

Water temperature: Bake time:

Humidity level: Length of bulk fermentation:

Describe how you feel as you begin baking your bread today:

_____

_____

What prayers, petitions, or thanksgivings are you bringing to God today?

_____

_____

_____

Describe how your dough looks and feels after your initial mix:

_____

_____

Describe how your dough looks and feels after the bulk fermentation:

_____

_____

Describe how your dough looks and feels during shaping:

_____

_____

Describe how your dough looks, feels, and tastes after baking and cooling:

_____

_____

How has God been present with you during today's bake?

_____

_____

Date:

Kitchen temperature: Start time:

Outside temperature: Shape time:

Water temperature: Bake time:

Humidity level: Length of bulk fermentation:

Describe how you feel as you begin baking your bread today:

_____

_____

What prayers, petitions, or thanksgivings are you bringing to God today?

_____

_____

_____

Describe how your dough looks and feels after your initial mix:

_____

_____

Describe how your dough looks and feels after the bulk fermentation:

_____

_____

Describe how your dough looks and feels during shaping:

_____

_____

Describe how your dough looks, feels, and tastes after baking and cooling:

_____

_____

How has God been present with you during today's bake?

_____

_____

_____

Date:

Kitchen temperature: Start time:

Outside temperature: Shape time:

Water temperature: Bake time:

Humidity level: Length of bulk fermentation:

Describe how you feel as you begin baking your bread today:

_____

_____

What prayers, petitions, or thanksgivings are you bringing to God today?

_____

_____

_____

Describe how your dough looks and feels after your initial mix:

_____

_____

Describe how your dough looks and feels after the bulk fermentation:

_____

_____

Describe how your dough looks and feels during shaping:

_____

_____

Describe how your dough looks, feels, and tastes after baking and cooling:

_____

_____

How has God been present with you during today's bake?

_____

_____

_____

Date:

Kitchen temperature: Start time:

Outside temperature: Shape time:

Water temperature: Bake time:

Humidity level: Length of bulk fermentation:

Describe how you feel as you begin baking your bread today:

_____

_____

What prayers, petitions, or thanksgivings are you bringing to God today?

_____

_____

_____

Describe how your dough looks and feels after your initial mix:

_____

_____

Describe how your dough looks and feels after the bulk fermentation:

_____

_____

Describe how your dough looks and feels during shaping:

_____

_____

Describe how your dough looks, feels, and tastes after baking and cooling:

_____

_____

How has God been present with you during today's bake?

_____

_____

_____

Date:

Kitchen temperature: Start time:

Outside temperature: Shape time:

Water temperature: Bake time:

Humidity level: Length of bulk fermentation:

Describe how you feel as you begin baking your bread today:

_____

_____

What prayers, petitions, or thanksgivings are you bringing to God today?

_____

_____

_____

Describe how your dough looks and feels after your initial mix:

_____

_____

Describe how your dough looks and feels after the bulk fermentation:

_____

_____

Describe how your dough looks and feels during shaping:

_____

_____

Describe how your dough looks, feels, and tastes after baking and cooling:

_____

_____

How has God been present with you during today's bake?

_____

_____

_____

Date:

Kitchen temperature: Start time:

Outside temperature: Shape time:

Water temperature: Bake time:

Humidity level: Length of bulk fermentation:

Describe how you feel as you begin baking your bread today:

_____

_____

What prayers, petitions, or thanksgivings are you bringing to God today?

_____

_____

_____

Describe how your dough looks and feels after your initial mix:

_____

_____

Describe how your dough looks and feels after the bulk fermentation:

_____

_____

Describe how your dough looks and feels during shaping:

_____

_____

Describe how your dough looks, feels, and tastes after baking and cooling:

_____

_____

How has God been present with you during today's bake?

_____

_____

_____

Date:

Kitchen temperature: Start time:

Outside temperature: Shape time:

Water temperature: Bake time:

Humidity level: Length of bulk fermentation:

Describe how you feel as you begin baking your bread today:

_____

_____

What prayers, petitions, or thanksgivings are you bringing to God today?

_____

_____

_____

Describe how your dough looks and feels after your initial mix:

_____

_____

Describe how your dough looks and feels after the bulk fermentation:

_____

_____

Describe how your dough looks and feels during shaping:

_____

_____

Describe how your dough looks, feels, and tastes after baking and cooling:

_____

_____

How has God been present with you during today's bake?

_____

_____

_____

Date:

Kitchen temperature: Start time:

Outside temperature: Shape time:

Water temperature: Bake time:

Humidity level: Length of bulk fermentation:

Describe how you feel as you begin baking your bread today:

_____

_____

What prayers, petitions, or thanksgivings are you bringing to God today?

_____

_____

_____

Describe how your dough looks and feels after your initial mix:

_____

_____

Describe how your dough looks and feels after the bulk fermentation:

_____

_____

Describe how your dough looks and feels during shaping:

_____

_____

Describe how your dough looks, feels, and tastes after baking and cooling:

_____

_____

How has God been present with you during today's bake?

_____

_____

_____

Date:

Kitchen temperature: Start time:

Outside temperature: Shape time:

Water temperature: Bake time:

Humidity level: Length of bulk fermentation:

Describe how you feel as you begin baking your bread today:

_____

_____

What prayers, petitions, or thanksgivings are you bringing to God today?

_____

_____

_____

Describe how your dough looks and feels after your initial mix:

_____

_____

Describe how your dough looks and feels after the bulk fermentation:

_____

_____

Describe how your dough looks and feels during shaping:

_____

_____

Describe how your dough looks, feels, and tastes after baking and cooling:

_____

_____

How has God been present with you during today's bake?

_____

_____

_____

Date:

Kitchen temperature: Start time:

Outside temperature: Shape time:

Water temperature: Bake time:

Humidity level: Length of bulk fermentation:

Describe how you feel as you begin baking your bread today:
_____
_____

What prayers, petitions, or thanksgivings are you bringing to God today?
_____
_____
_____

Describe how your dough looks and feels after your initial mix:
_____
_____

Describe how your dough looks and feels after the bulk fermentation:
_____
_____

Describe how your dough looks and feels during shaping:
_____
_____

Describe how your dough looks, feels, and tastes after baking and cooling:
_____
_____

How has God been present with you during today's bake?
_____
_____
_____

Glossary of Baking Terms

ACTIVE DRY YEAST: *see yeast*

AUTOLYZE: a short rest after flour and water has been mixed that allows the flour to hydrate and gluten bonds to form

BRAN: the outer shell of a wheat kernel containing a high volume of fiber

BREAD FLOUR: a high-protein flour suitable for making bread, typically made using a hard spring wheat

BULK FERMENTATION: the long fermentation when most of the flavor and texture develop in dough

CAKE YEAST: *see yeast*

COLD FERMENTATION: *see fermentation*

FERMENTATION: the process of sugars being broken down into alcohols using bacteria and yeast. When bread is made, the carbon dioxide byproduct of fermentation is trapped in gluten strands, which raises the dough. This fermentation can take place at room temperature, or it can be slowed down by letting the dough rest at a colder temperature, such as in a refrigerator. The longer, colder fermentation develops more flavor in the dough.

FRESH YEAST: *see yeast*

GERM: the portion of wheat responsible for reproduction and containing a large quantity of fat

GLUTEN: the protein in wheat made up of glutenin and gliadin. As the amino acids form bonds with one another, they create a strong protein network that captures carbon dioxide gas to serve as the backbone of the bread.

HIGH-HYDRATION DOUGH: dough made with a high ratio of water to flour

INSTANT YEAST: *see yeast*

PROOF: also called a rise, this is a rest during which the yeast "proves" it is still alive by growing the dough a little more

SEMOLINA: a coarse flour made of the high-protein durum variety of wheat; often used in making pasta

SOURDOUGH: dough leavened using a culture of wild bacteria and yeast rather than commercial yeast

SPROUTED-WHEAT FLOUR: flour made from wheat that has sprouted. The kernels have been allowed to begin the process of growing into a plant, then halted, dehydrated, and ground into flour. This process activates enzymes that make the grains more digestible and flavorful.

WINDOWPANE TEST: a test for determining whether enough gluten has developed in a batch of bread dough. Cut off a small piece of dough, then stretch it between your fingers. When the gluten is fully formed, you should be able to stretch it thin enough to hold it up to a light and see the light shine through.

YEAST: In the United States, commercial yeast is typically available from the grocery store in granulated form. Instant, or rapid rise, yeast and active dry yeast are both dehydrated versions of *Saccharomyces cerevisiae*, though the first is ground more finely. I like to think of these types of yeast as being a morning person versus . . . not a morning person. Instant yeast is awake and ready to leaven as soon as it's mixed with flour and water. That means it can typically be mixed directly into the dough. Active dry yeast needs a slower start to its day: a long soak in water and a breakfast of sugar or honey to liven it up before it's ready to get to work in the flour. In a high-hydration, long-fermentation dough, such as the Bake & Pray loaf, the slow fermentation makes up for the difference in speed between the two, which means they can be used interchangeably. Fresh yeast, also known as cake yeast, is *Saccharomyces cerevisiae* that hasn't been dehydrated or ground into granules. It is prevalent across the Commonwealth but difficult to find in the United States.

Acknowledgments

EVERY BOOK IS A MIRACLE, BORN OUT OF COMMUNITY—a community of those who encourage and support the author, shaping her thoughts as she works them out on the page, and a community of editors, designers, publishers, and more who make it possible for you to hold the book in your hands.

Thank you to the many communities that have supported me in the writing of this book, especially my dear friends Kaitlyn Schiess and Emily Fiedler, who have spent more hours at my dinner table, listening to me ramble through my anxieties and my joys, than probably anyone else in the world.

KC, Jess, Carlynn, and Esther, my food studies ladies; Abby, Kate, and Jessica, who encourage me constantly through our daily writing check-ins; Emily and Gabrielle, who have witnessed this Bake & Pray journey from the very beginning; Amanda Windes and Amanda Opelt, Tamara and Seth, Claire and Charlie, Kat, Hannah, Aminah, Christina, and so many more, who have tasted countless recipes and helped me in my research and just generally encouraged me every step of the way: I am so grateful for all of you.

To all those who have been part of the Edible Theology community over the years: it's because of you I get to write a book like this one! A special thanks to Edible Theology's board members (and my good friends) Kayla Hopgood, Margarita Diaz Lutz, and Jerusalem Greer, and to the team of recipe testers who ensured each recipe in this book is ready for baking: Amanda Cox, Amy McEntee, Ayanna Kafi Stringer, Caroline Robicsek, Daniel Pons, Elizabeth Brewington, Emma Mueller, Emily Cowser, Emily Dalen, Ginny Masterson, Hannah Bunting, Janice Johnson, Joann Felker, Katie Lowe, Lisa Hammershaimb, Maddie Johnson, Mallory Coffey, Michele Somerville, Nancy Lee Gauche, Nichelle Walters, Stephanie Buchan, Suzanne Kabisch, and Tamisyn Grantz.

Thank you to my agent, Lisa Jackson of Alive Literary, and to the entire team at Tyndale: Kara Leonino, Stephanie Rische, Julie Chen, Sarah Atkinson, and Madeline Daniels. I'm thankful that you all were willing to take a risk on a strange concept for a devotional and that you came alongside me every step of the way!

To Alyssa, Scott, Griffin, and Avery; Davis and Jessica; Emma Claire and Isaiah: I'm so grateful you are my family. And to my parents, Doug and Angela: thank you for your prayers and your endless support along this strange but beautiful Edible Theology career. I love you.

Notes

INTRODUCTION

1. Eugene Peterson, *Eat This Book: A Conversation in the Art of Spiritual Reading* (Grand Rapids, MI: Eerdmans, 2009).

PART 2: BASICS OF BREAD

1. Adapted from Kendall Vanderslice, "Remember, You Are Flour," Kendall Vanderslice (blog), March 1, 2017, http://kendallvanderslice.com/blog/remember-you-are-flour.
2. Thomas Merton, *Thoughts in Solitude* (New York: Farrar, Straus and Giroux, 1999), 79.
3. Adele Costabile et al, "Effect of Breadmaking Process on *In Vitro* Gut Microbiota Parameters in Irritable Bowel Syndrome," PLOS ONE 9(10): e111225 (October 30, 2014), https://doi.org/10.1371/journal.pone.0111225.
4. Abraham Joshua Heschel, *The Sabbath* (New York: Farrar Straus Giroux, 2005).
5. Peter Reinhart, "The Art and Craft of Bread," Filmed July 2008 in St. Helena, CA, TED video, 15:14, https://www.ted.com/talks/peter_reinhart_the_art_and_craft_of_bread/transcript?language=en.

PART 4: RECIPES FOR THE CHURCH YEAR

1. Fleming Rutledge, *Advent: The Once and Future Coming of Jesus Christ* (Grand Rapids, MI: Eerdmans, 2018), 7.
2. Sam O'Brien, "Detangling the Devilish Origins of Scandinavia's St. Lucia Buns," *Gastro Obscura*, December 11, 2020, https://www.atlasobscura.com/articles/st-lucia-day-buns.
3. Andreja Brulc, "Mexico Project: Mexican Cuisine: Pan Dulce," Andreja Brulc's blog, October 31, 2013, https://andrejabrulc.wordpress.com/2013/10/31/mexico-project-mexican-cuisine-pan-dulce-sweet-bread/
4. Paul F. Bradshaw and Maxwell E. Johnson, *The Origins of Feasts, Fasts, and Seasons in Early Christianity* (Collegeville, MN: Liturgical Press, 2011).

6. Dresdner Christstollen, https://www.dresdnerstollen.com/en/dresdner-christstollen.
7. Tony, Kavalieros, "Christopsomo—The Bread of Christ," *The Greek Chef* (blog), https://thegreekchef.us/blog/christopsomo-the-bread-of-christ/.
8. "A Brief History of the Moravian Church," The Moravian Church, https://www.moravian.org/2018/07/a-brief-history-of-the-moravian-church/.
9. Father Milan Savich, "The Meaning of Fasting in the Orthodox Church," The Antiochian Orthodox Christian Archdiocese of North America, http://ww1.antiochian.org/node/50791.

About the Author

KENDALL VANDERSLICE is a baker, writer, and speaker, as well as the founder of the Edible Theology Project, a ministry that connects the Communion table to the kitchen table. She is a graduate of Wheaton College (BA anthropology), Boston University (MLA gastronomy), and Duke Divinity School (master of theological studies). Her bylines include *Christianity Today*, *Bitter Southerner*, *Christian Century*, *Religion News Service*, and *Faith and Leadership*. She is the author of *By Bread Alone* and *We Will Feast*. Kendall lives (with her big-eared beagle named Strudel) in Durham, North Carolina, where she teaches workshops on bread baking as a spiritual practice. Visit her online at kendallvanderslice.com.

ALSO BY
KENDALL VANDERSLICE

In *By Bread Alone,* Kendall weaves her own faith-filled journey together with original recipes and stories about the role of bread in church history, revealing a God who draws near to us and creatively provides for our daily needs in the sacred and the mundane.

AVAILABLE WHEREVER BOOKS ARE SOLD.